The Lazy Gardener

The Lazy Gardener

Mara Grey

Illustrations by Vasily Kafanov

GRAMERCY BOOKS
New York

This 2002 edition is published by Gramercy Books™, an imprint of Random House Value Publishing, Inc., 280 Park Avenue, New York, NY 10017, by arrangement with Macmillan Publishing.

Gramercy Books™ and design are trademarks of Random House Value Publishing, Inc.

Random House
New York • Toronto • London • Sydney • Auckland
http://www.randomhouse.com/

Printed and bound in the United States of America

Library of Congress Cataloging-in-Publication Data
Grey, Mara.
    The lazy gardener / Mara Grey ; illustrations by Vasily Kafanov.
        p. cm.
    Originally published: New York, NY : Macmillan, c1998.
    ISBN 0-517-21994-8 (alk. paper)
        1. Gardening. 2. Low maintenance gardening. I. Title.

    SB453 .G84 2002
    635.9—dc21

                                                    2001050169

10 9 8 7 6 5 4 3 2 1

Contents

Part Three: Getting Your Hands in the Dirt ◆ 85

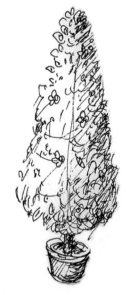

Introduction

Are You a Lazy Gardener?

D o you qualify as a lazy gardener? Do you, consciously or unconsciously, treat your plants as though they are capable of surviving on their own? Do you go hiking instead of setting up the sprinkler, watch butterflies instead of weeding, or romp with your kids instead of mowing the lawn?

Do you want to be surrounded by a garden as beautiful as a mountain meadow, with its acres of flowers, spicy scents, and fascinating textures? Like a mountain meadow, does your ideal garden take care of itself? No weeding, no watering, no spraying for bugs?

Stand up and admit it. You're a Lazy Gardener. So am I.

We tend to feel guilty about our gardening sins, about what we've learned to call neglect. We "should" mow the lawn, we "should" water the shrubs, we "should" get the weeds out of the raspberries.

Our gardening has become so burdened with "shoulds" that we see nothing else when we look out the window. The peony buds about to unfold and the forget-me-nots surrounding our doorstep are ignored.

Our chores, our "shoulds," are necessary at times, but why would anyone confuse them with the true harvest of gardening, the appreciation of small miracles surrounding us?

What would happen if we were honest about our inability to take on the role of "nursemaid"? Is that such a terrible thing to admit? Our gardens are places where we encounter nature in detail. Do you want a relationship of equality or one of domination?

Let's start off by making a serious assault on our guilt, changing the term for our attitude from neglect to respect. Respect? Yes. Most traditional gardening methods are based on a view of nature as something to be conquered, controlled: Many of the perfect gardens you see in magazine pictures exemplify this confrontational viewpoint. Our neglect may actually stem from a conviction that our friendship with nature shouldn't involve strange rituals like spraying for disease five times a year.

Gardening with respect is gardening from the heart. It gives us the freedom to observe and accept whatever happens around us, even the slug that destroyed one of our lettuce plants or the slow disease that killed our fir. Gardening with respect doesn't negate our own feelings and desires. We have the ability to choose, to say, "I'm not having any quack grass" or "I love roses and I'm going to have roses."

However, as lazy gardeners, we agree to accept the earth as a partner in a game of give and take, rather than flatten her with an urge to have everything our own way. We have respect.

My own break with gardening tradition first came when I found beetles chewing the tips off my young asparagus plants. I sat down to watch, fascinated by the process. After a few minutes, I realized that I couldn't choose between the beetles and my future dinner. Perhaps it was my biologist's training; perhaps it was simply laziness. Whatever the reason, I needed to accept them both.

Now, this kind of attitude can play havoc with gardening life—especially vegetable gardening. Most vegetables are simply not suited to being treated as wild plants. The truly lazy gardener, however, would live on an abundance of dandelions, chickweed, and nettles, rich in minerals and eager to grow almost anywhere.

I haven't arrived at that point yet, and you probably haven't either. There are degrees of willingness to accommodate nature. Lazy gardening is a journey, an exploration, not a fixed destination. Perhaps you're just on the edge of being a lazy gardener, or you are getting ready to take the plunge, having had enough of "too much work and not enough time to do it." If so, this book is for you.

—Mara Grey

A Quick Quiz

HELP!!! I'm Too Busy to Read This Book!

There are two ways to use *The Lazy Gardener*: read it from cover to cover, or use the following quiz to help you identify the information you need most. Each statement or question below is paired with a corresponding page number (or page numbers) in the text. To start off, simply check the three to four sentences that seem the most relevant to your situation and look up the solutions (you can always come back for more).

Planning

- ❏ I like gardens, but my own is such a muddle. I just can't decide what to do with it. (p. 3)
- ❏ Can I really draw up a plan on my own? (p. 27)
- ❏ I'm no artist, but I want colors that work together. (p. 36)
- ❏ I want some privacy. What about fences and hedges? (p. 42)
- ❏ I would like pots on my deck. (p. 56)
- ❏ I like those pictures of English gardens, overflowing with flowers, but aren't they a lot of work? (p. 53)
- ❏ I want a lush-looking garden with tall plants, but don't want to bother with stakes. (p. 59)
- ❏ I fall in love with almost every plant I see, but I'll leave plant collections to botanical gardens. How do I choose? (p. 21)
- ❏ I need a tree to shade my deck. How do I choose one? (p. 63)
- ❏ Fresh vegetables sound great, but I haven't got the time to grow them. (p. 69)
- ❏ I want lots of birds, butterflies, and frogs in my garden. (p. 75)

❑ I want my garden to be a place of peace and connection with nature. (p. 81)

Help!

❑ I'm just starting out and don't have any tools. What do I need to buy? (p. 135)
❑ I've got a plan for my yard, but where do I start? (p. 114)
❑ I've just built a house and there's a quarter acre of dust (or mud) surrounding me. (p. 111)
❑ I want the garden to fill in fast. (p. 64)
❑ I don't have much money to spend on plants. (p. 39)
❑ I'm overwhelmed. I need boundaries. (p. 35)
❑ I feel so guilty about all the plants that have died, all the projects waiting to be finished, and all the things I could have done that I can't get started. (p. 87)
❑ I hate weeding! I haven't pulled a weed in a year and they're starting to climb the front steps. (p. 123)
❑ I love plants, but all I want to do when I get home is hide inside. All I see in my garden is hours of work that need doing. (p. 93)
❑ All the seedlings I put out get eaten by slugs or snails or something. Help! (p. 129)
❑ I don't like chemical sprays, but my favorite tree is under attack. What do I do? (p. 130)
❑ I love roses (or dahlias or sweet peas), but they always get one disease or another. Help! (p. 132)
❑ I know August isn't a good time to transplant, but my neighbor said I could have the shrubs he's hauling out. How do I give them a good start? (p. 101)

What's Going on Here?

❑ I don't know the first thing about soil. How do I know what I've got and what to do with it? (p. 13)
❑ What about watering? When, how much, and why? (pp. 8, 102)
❑ How do I choose a fertilizer? (p. 103)
❑ Every time I prune something it looks like a wreck. How do I do it right? (p. 105)
❑ How do I seed, divide, and take cuttings? (p. 107)
❑ I just bought a flat of petunias, three roses, and a maple. How do I plant them? (p. 99)
❑ Why does everyone tell me to mulch? (p. 46)
❑ Would a ground cover really keep down the weeds? (p. 47)
❑ How do I build a pond? (p. 77)
❑ I don't know much about what grows well in my area. How can I get some good advice? (p. 22)
❑ How do I choose the healthiest plants? (p. 23)

PART ONE

The Big Picture

Gardens are shaped by details, by hundreds of decisions and choices. Which perennial on the nursery table would look best next to the back door? Do I plant carrots or potatoes? Do I weed this morning or in three weeks?

All these details can seem overwhelming until placed within the context of your own personal plan, your vision, and an understanding of how plants and gardens work. When you see where you're going and how nature can help or hinder you, you can put in minimum effort for maximum effect.

Chapter One

What's a Garden for, Anyway?

irst things first. Why are you going to all the trouble to make a garden? Why don't you just pave the whole yard or plant a green lawn and hire someone else to mow it? What do you want to get out of all this work?

Gardens are seductive—especially the perfectly pruned gardens in glossy photographs or the fantasy gardens of our imagination. We'd feel content with life, with ourselves, just walking around in such an ideal garden. We'd be surrounded by fragrance, color, and beauty. Of course we want one!

Once enthralled by these images, we become vulnerable to the instructions surrounding them. "You need these plants." "You need to improve the soil." "You must fertilize every six weeks." "Bait for slugs." "Good gardeners don't have weeds."

To combat these and other commands from traditional gardening sources, you need to pinpoint what it is you want and look for alternative ways to get it. The look of abundance pictured in a book doesn't necessarily have to come from peonies and delphiniums. If that's your delight, figure out how to get it with plants that don't need staking. (To find out how, see p. 59.)

First, pull out a piece of paper and write down your answers to the question "Why do I want a garden?" Be honest, now, and—for the moment—forget practicalities. If you really want to impress the neighbors, fine. If you want a place to sit naked in the sun, fine. If you want

3

to attract birds, fine. Or perhaps you want a garden just like Grandma's. Think about what would make you happiest: A compliment from Aunt Bess? Being able to grow a particular plant for which you have a passion? Parties on the lawn? Hosting a particular species of woodpecker?

Each reason, each role, calls for a different strategy, a unique plan to get what you want. A garden to impress the neighbors, for instance, calls for an openness to view; a garden for lolling around naked demands screening. Perhaps both of these desires could be satisfied by creating a display garden in the front yard and a private one in the back.

Enthusiasm is the only true motivator for lazy gardeners, and connecting with your desires is the only way to fulfill them. Who would put hours of work into a boring project? Yet what's boring to one is exciting to another. This is your garden. Do it your way.

Again, forget practicalities. The rest of this book deals with getting what you want with a minimum amount of work. You'd be surprised at how easily you can impress your neighbors or Aunt Bess. The most important step is to choose the right strategy. And you can't do that until you know what you want to accomplish, until you have a sense of direction and purpose.

This brainstorming exercise will encourage you to clear out the farfetched ideas first, so you can open the door to new possibilities. Perhaps you never considered a totally private backyard. Perhaps a desire for sensuous abundance lurks beneath your no-nonsense, practical exterior. Doodle a bit. Think about all the gardens you've seen. What did you like about them? Wait for a new desire to announce itself.

A garden can be a place to relax, a beautiful setting for your home, a space for volleyball games or for kids to play hide-and-seek, a wildlife sanctuary, or space for a collection of rare plants. It can even be a place to exercise your creativity, much like building sand castles and miniature landscapes when you were a kid.

When you run out of images that excite you, put your paper away for a few days. Let your subconscious go to work. You may find yourself suddenly drawn to one image that popped up, or you may elaborate a scene by daydreaming about it. Or you may realize that something you thought was important really doesn't matter.

Patience is a lazy gardener's best friend. I've seen more gardens ruined by hasty planting than by anything else. In fact, most garden problems can be traced to impulse buying, poor planning, and impatience. Take your time; nature's rhythms are slow.

Now, while you're in the gestation period, broaden your perspective to include the question "What relationship do I want to create with the earth?" This garden, this bit of land, is your laboratory for one-on-one encounters with nature, with all the challenges we face in working with the earth as a whole.

Do we spray asparagus beetles with pesticides, find a nontoxic way of getting rid of them, or accept them as fellow travelers? Which alternative will give us the most free time? Which one gives us the asparagus we want to eat? Can we have both?

Gardens have always reflected prevailing views of humanity's place in nature. Look at the formal French grounds around Versailles, in which nature is subservient. Or the romantic English gardens of the nineteenth century, which idealized nature but employed teams of gardeners to create the illusion of it. Or Japanese gardens, created as carefully controlled symbolic works of art.

Small suburban gardens have always drawn on these traditions, using them as models and inspiration. Open lawns recall manor grounds. Three carefully tended rosebushes re-create a formal garden in miniature. No one pointed out that the great gardens on which these smaller versions are based were created by people who hired professional gardeners to do the work.

One person I met recently told me of going to a talk given by a popular garden writer. When asked about a certain disease, she said, "Oh, I just let my gardeners take care of that." He almost stood up and said, "In my garden, I'm the only gardener! What do I do when I can't delegate the duties?"

If we can't delegate, we have to be smart. We have to pay attention to nature's cues. That's what being a lazy gardener is all about.

NARROW IT DOWN: WHAT DO YOU REALLY WANT?

After completing the exercises in the last section, you have some gut feelings, some excitement building for things that could happen in your garden. Now let's get down to the details.

The first step is to answer the question "Who are you?" What do you know about yourself and your desires? How can you enter into a partnership with a garden if you're fuzzy about yourself, living in a world of what you'd like to be?

That's the key. Don't plan on changing yourself, or the rest of your life. Yes, if you were well organized, retired, and very wealthy, you'd create a garden just like pictures in the books, but here you are, right now. Your bank balance is low, chaos is your middle name, and you can hardly find time for a night out, much less time in your garden. Whatever you've got, whoever you are, that's the starting point. That's the person who is going to create a garden.

Do you love to have flowers around, but are you not too particular about what kind they are? Do you want to grow food? Do you just want something to cover the ground and look fairly neat?

We'll be looking at lazy ways to fulfill your wishes in later chapters. Just remember to choose goals that respect the natural processes of your place as much as possible. In other words, don't fight the bugs, work around them.

But first, try another exercise. Write the words "My Garden" in the center of a page. All around this statement, begin to jot down single words or phrases taken from the garden wish list you created earlier—for example, beauty, impressing the neighbors, lying naked in the sun—and connect them by lines to "My Garden" in the center.

Next, consider each topic and branch off from it. "Beauty," for instance, might give birth to "lots of flowers," "fall color," "roses," "maple tree," and even "a honeysuckle like Grandma had."

"Lying naked in the sun" could lead to thoughts of "a fence or hedge," "a soft lawn to lie on," and "trees in front of the neighbor's second-story windows." Again, throw out practicality: This is pure, impulsive brainstorming.

And remember that none of these scenarios is mutually exclusive. You can usually have everything you want by setting aside certain areas for one function or another, or by planning through the seasons. Sunbathing is generally a summer activity, supported by thick, leafy growth. Spring could be your time to impress the neighbors with exuberant blooms.

Keep going until the torrent of ideas slows to a trickle. Then put it away for a few days. Chances are a few important wishes will surface while you're driving or taking a shower. Get them down on the paper, then take a good look at what you've got. Is it overwhelming? Or do you suddenly realize what's truly important to you?

The Bottom Line

Prioritizing is useful, especially when deciding where to start spending time and money. Just remember that the highest priority is the one that gets the kid in you excited and eager to begin, the one that seems like the most fun.

Often this will be the most visible project, the bed next to the front door or along the path you walk every day. Go for immediate rewards when you can. Redoing the back left corner of the garden may hardly make a difference to your mood; placing a few pots of annuals by the front door may perk up your day in minutes.

But don't do anything just yet. This exercise is like a seed planted in fertile ground. It needs time to grow, to put down roots and develop a few small leaves. Insights, ways to get what you need, and shifts in priorities will keep coming to you.

Perhaps it's the right kind of fence that you happen to see on sale a few weeks later. Or the gift of a special rose from the garden of a friend who doesn't really like the color. Trust your garden to grow itself, underground, before you go out and start pushing.

Grow itself? Yes. Gardens, strangely enough, seem to germinate, sprout, and bud in the same way that plants do. We're not always in control. Oh, of course we plan, devise strategies, choose directions. But there are always undercurrents, upwellings, the spirit of another creator taking a hand. Call it God, the earth, or the universe—we always encounter a partner in our inventing. Wait and watch for help.

While you're waiting, use your notes to create a file of hopes, loves, and delights. Clip pictures that inspire you. Do you want a pond? Love roses? Cut a few photos out of a catalog or magazine. This is good winter work, well suited to sitting in front of a fire during a storm. Always remember to have fun; if it becomes a chore, stop.

After a few weeks, start thinking about how much time you want to spend creating this garden. A day every week? An hour a week? An hour a month? Would you rather just hire someone to do everything?

Now consider the rest of your life, including your family, your job, your best friend's dinner parties, skiing vacations, and who knows what else. How much time can you reasonably expect to grab from an already overcrowded life? Now cut this figure in half.

Half? Yes. Indoor enthusiasm, or a table of brilliantly colored flowers at the nursery center, induces optimism—which is fine in itself, but no basis for planning a garden. The lavish display you envision and the spare minutes you're sure you'll have are like the deep end of the pool. Don't jump in over your head.

So now you realize that a few hours a month are just about right. A hopeless situation? No. What you've just identified is the amount of time you can spend on maintenance, on routine weeding, watering, and tidying up. These are chores we can minimize. The major work is in planning and setting up each bed, each a one-time project that can be scheduled in when you have a few days free.

The perfect garden for a lazy gardener is, paradoxically, a bit of work for awhile. If you want long-term savings on maintenance, you need to put in mulch and ground covers, and keep them well weeded until they fill in. You need to water even drought-resistant plants for a year or two.

So, a time budget for a neglectable garden actually has three columns: setting up new beds (most of your time), maintaining newly set up beds (less time), and maintaining mature beds (almost no time). Schedule your main chunks of planting for fall or spring, when rain can take care of most of the watering. The rest of the year, do whatever you can to retain your advances: Weed and fertilize when you must.

The best way to minimize setup time, as well as financial investment, is to work your garden in very small chunks. There is no recipe for disaster like planting a whole yard all at once. If you can afford to hire help for awhile, fine.

You can pay for professional advice in the planning stage, but be sure the person you listen to is knowledgeable about low-maintenance,

Chores That Can Be Fun and Creative

Pruning, especially shaping a neglected tree into a beautiful form

Mulching, because the garden looks so good afterward

Choosing places to put new plants

Dividing plants, replanting in clumps

Moving plants, creating new combinations

Cutting a neat edge in a neglected bed

Boring, Tedious Jobs Best Delegated or Avoided

Pulling quack grass

Watering

Mowing the lawn

Staking weak stems

Removing sod

Spraying for insects or disease

drought-resistant plantings. Many landscape architects and designers have brilliant, creative ideas for garden layout, but have little experience with plants or tend to use a repertoire of plants familiar to them, chosen for design considerations, not toughness.

Hiring someone to get you through the biggest jobs, perhaps clearing an area you want to redesign, is probably your best investment. Save all the best work for yourself and delegate the boring chores to others if you can.

If you can't afford help, cultivate patience and focus. Patience is the essential fruit of lazy gardening, costing little in time or money. Impulse buying is always a threat to those of us who fall in love with a dozen plants on any trip to a nursery. Impulsive project starting is another disease that makes random attacks. Both clog a garden's natural flow. With patience, knowledge, and the right techniques you can have everything that is truly important to you.

Chapter Two

Your Basic Ingredients: Sun, Soil, Water, Air

Look at your yard from a plant's point of view. If you were a tree, what would you need? As a seed ready to sprout, you would need water to keep you moist and soil to anchor your first roots. When your first leaves unfold, you need the sun to give you warmth and energy to start food production, photosynthesis. You need air to surround roots and leaves with oxygen and carbon dioxide.

Simple? Perhaps. Some plants are picky, refusing to grow unless they have the right mix, while others, such as dandelions and bracken fern, make do with anything. Some come from deserts, some from southern bogs, some from rocky northern forests. Whether they settle into your garden successfully depends on how closely you can match water, soil, air, and sun to their needs. Here is their wish list to pair with your own.

SUN

Sunlight is vital. Plants use it to manufacture carbohydrates and food. Leaves and branches seek light, stretching upward and outward to find it. Without enough, plants literally starve to death.

Different kinds of plants have different light needs. Some can survive in the constant shade of a forest floor. At the other extreme, some require the intense sun found only in a high desert.

Often, the shape, size, and color of plants' leaves will give you clues as to their preferences. Small, gray woolly leaves are adapted to strong sun; large, thin, bright green leaves are usually light gatherers that need shade.

If a plant is getting too much sun, its leaves may burn on the edges in random brown splotches. They can also shrink and turn yellowish, sometimes curling under in an effort to reduce their size.

Plants getting too little sun are weak, spindly, and lopsided, from stretching too eagerly toward the light. Flowers are absent, sometimes even when the plant itself looks healthy.

Patterns of light change dramatically from winter to summer. Ideally, you would spend a year just observing these changes. When do the new leaves on the maple shade the bed beneath? When does the north side of the house start getting some sun? How many hours a day does the east side get in March? In July? The more keen your observation, the more appropriate your planting will be.

Remember that shade has many dimensions, from the shifting light patterns beneath a fine-leaved maple to the gloom created by a large fir on the north side of a house. Overcast days, surprisingly, may provide extra indirect illumination for plants next to walls.

The sun also provides warmth, and each plant has its range of tolerance for heat, or lack of it. You can get local information on common minimum winter temperatures, date of last frost, and so on, but individual gardens have their idiosyncracies.

Again, try to spend a year just observing these patterns before planting anything. Where is the warmest spot in midsummer? Where does frost or snow melt last? These are spots to treat with care. The first one may be just right for tomatoes or a southern shrub; the second demands cast-iron hardiness in anything planted there.

While some gardeners build greenhouses, lath houses, or plastic tents to outwit frost or change the climate around a melon vine, you're better off avoiding the plants that need them. Stop thinking of "good" gardening as battling the elements; better gardens work around them.

SOIL AND THE ROOTS IT SURROUNDS

The first thing a seed does when it sprouts is push a single root downward into the ground, searching for stability, for a moist but oxygen-rich environment to explore. Single-cell-thick root hairs, vulnerable to the slightest breath of dry air, soak up water and the nutrients dissolved in it. Some plants can get by with less oxygen in the soil, some with fewer nutrients. The key is to match your garden with plants that would consider its conditions ideal. So dig down a couple of feet and look at what you have to work with. Try a couple of places in your yard; soil can change over short distances.

pH Values

The first thing you'll want to know is the pH value of your soil. This is shorthand for the degree of acidity or alkalinity: A pH of 7 is neutral; pH values between 0 and 7 indicate acidity, 0 being the most acidic; pH values between 7 and 14 indicate alkalinity, 14 being the most alkaline. The pH is usually produced by a combination of the climate and the native vegetation that produced the soil.

Test kits from your local garden store are fine for getting a general sense of your soil's pH, though results are not as accurate as those from a soil-testing laboratory. Your county extention agent can help you with advice on whether or not you'll need more elaborate analysis. Often the soil in an area has uniform characteristics and unless you're a commercial vegetable grower you won't need exact information on potassium or phosphorous content.

In the Pacific Northwest, for instance, soil is usually acidic because of the high rainfall and the continuous existence of ancient conifer forests. A deciduous forest or grass plain produces soil close to neutral; deserts tend to be alkaline.

Most plants will grow well in neutral or slightly acid soil; they will even thrive in a mildly alkaline soil. Some plants, however, require acidity. These include cranberries, strawberries, blueberries, camellias, rhododendrons, azaleas, kalmia, and potatoes. If your soil tests above pH 7, delete them from your list or be prepared to dig in lots of organic matter, which will lower the pH. Peat moss, which is dug from bogs, is especially good for this purpose.

If your soil tests below pH 6, you can add ground limestone to raise pH, or specialize in the plants listed above. Limestone is a slow-acting amendment, so give it a few months to start dissolving before you plant.

Some Soil Preferences

Carrots: even-textured, somewhat sandy soil, without much nitrogen

Oriental poppies (*Papaver orientale*): ordinary, well-draining soil, without fertilizer

Bearded iris: can take clay soil if well drained, not picky about pH

Clematis: soils close to neutral with added calcium, mulched to provide coolness for the roots

Wisteria: well-draining soil not excessively acidic or alkaline

Forsythia: not picky about soil pH or texture

Camellia: well-draining acidic soil high in organic matter

Pine (*Pinus*): ordinary to poor soil with good drainage

Soil Texture

Now check the texture of your sample. Sandy soil is usually light-colored and drains water quickly. Clay soil is sticky and drains poorly. Rub a bit between your fingers. If it feels gritty, then you've got some sand. Does it feel smooth, clinging to your skin? This means you have a lot of clay, fragments of minerals that pack together tightly, leaving little space for air or water to enter.

Most soils also have some organic matter in them. This is a broad term that covers anything from half-rotted leaves and dead bugs to the sticky black end-product of decay called humus. Organic matter is like a sponge, absorbing water and nutrients that might wash right through the root area and storing them until needed. A highly organic soil can hoard 10 to 15 times more water than one with just minerals.

Obviously, a sandy soil stays moist longer with added organics. What isn't so obvious is how clay soils benefit. These hold water well but have few air spaces, and they cling to water so tightly that plants have difficulty extracting it. Organic matter opens up clay soils and binds the minerals together to make larger, sand- or silt-sized particles. The result is better drainage, with more oxygen getting to the roots.

If you have a mixture of sand, clay, and medium-sized particles, with some organic matter darkening the concoction, you're lucky. Most plants will thrive there. If your soil mix is tilted in one direction or the other, you can choose plants that like that kind of soil or put in some work to change it.

Amending the Soil

Change the soil only if you must. Creating a pocket of rich soil, a banquet for the roots, tends to tempt them to stay at the table instead of reaching out. You'll have wide, healthy root systems if you don't baby them.

Some exceptions are rhododendrons and azaleas, whose fibrous, compact root systems need highly organic soil. Consider the needs also of container-grown plants that have had a rich diet and may appreciate an intermediate stage. But always try to match the plant with the soil, rather than the other way around.

There are, however, three situations demanding major soil renovation. First, if you've just built a new house and the heavy construction equipment has compacted the ground, you will have to loosen it again. If the top soil has been stripped off and all you have left is sand and gravel, you need to take emergency measures before you can plant anything.

Second, if you have heavy clay soil, you'll have to add organic matter to be able to grow much of anything. Yes, there are plants that like clay, but you'll have to take your choice between the work of digging in organic matter and the limitations clay will put on your plant selection.

Third, if you're planting for drought resistance in a desert, the extra effort to dig deep into the soil and add moisture-holding organic material makes sense.

If you need to improve the soil, what do you do? The easiest, though not the quickest, way is to plant winter rye, a grain whose far-ranging root system will break up compact soil, gather clay minerals together into easy-to-work-with crumbs, and add lots of moisture-holding humus to the soil. When the leaves are about six inches high, you dig the rye under, then plant it again.

If you need a faster method, choose whatever material is cheapest in your area (see sidebar) and use a lot of it. Spread it three or four inches thick, then dig it in as deeply as you can. While you're at it, add some extras like bone meal, manure, and seaweed. Homemade compost is wonderful, too, if you enjoy making it; see p. 104 for an easy method. Doing a thorough job will at least give you a sense of satisfaction in payment for your labor. Refer to Chapter 15, p. 99, to learn more about amendments and fertilizers for healthy plants.

Soil for Containers

Plants in pots and other containers need light, fast-draining soils that also hold water. Lots of organic matter and weightless amendments such as perlite are called for here. I distrust most packaged soils, finding that they have too much peat, which hardens and sheds water when dry. I buy the mix but add mushroom compost, fine bark, and a little steer manure, then store it in a garbage can. It takes a few minutes to mix, but is handy for any potting needed later.

WATER

No one runs around with a watering hose in the wilderness, so plants have evolved ways to survive with the unpredictable, sometimes meager, supply nature provides. Regular oversupplies have been adapted to as well.

Many wild plants began their gardening careers in England, whose moist, even climate shaped our image of the modern garden. For many years nurseries carried only varieties suited to this imagery, not to the land on which we live. However, that is changing.

Drought-resistant plants aren't limited to cactus and spiny shrubs. Intricate textures and bright, even flamboyant, colors fill gardens whose hoses see little use.

Why do plants need water? Like us, their bodies are mostly water, and also like us, they are constantly losing it. Without a new supply,

Cheap Organic Materials—Some Possibilities

Stable manure mixed with sawdust or straw (make sure there are no weed seeds included)

Composted city pruning and lawn waste

Sawdust (add slow-release nitrogen amendment to compensate for loss during decay)

Sawdust mixed with grass clippings

Pine needles (acidic, add ground limestone)

Fallen leaves

Ground sugarcane

Cocoa shells

Ground corncobs

Peanut shells

most will quickly shrivel and collapse. Water also carries dissolved nutrients to be used in building tissue.

Where and when does water fall on your garden? You could get an average rainfall figure from the weather bureau, but only observation will give you a sense of the particular patterns in your own yard. Which spots are sheltered by walls or overhangs? Where does runoff pool? How long does it take to wet the soil underneath the oak in the back corner? Are there places that don't dry out at all until June? Are there difficult-to-water slopes? Is there any place you can't reach with a hose? Are there any willows or other trees whose roots rob the soil of water?

The first step in any watering strategy is to make the best use of what falls naturally. You want all the water to seep into the ground; none should puddle or run off. Drops striking bare soil dry to create a thin compacted layer called a crust, which keeps the next rain from soaking in. Mulch or create a ground cover, and this problem will be gone.

Mulches or ground covers also keep the surface of the soil from losing water. (See p. 45 for more information on mulches and ground covers.) While the leaves of the ground cover lose water during photosynthesis, unless you live in a desert, this shouldn't outweigh the advantages of a permanent, self-perpetuating shield for the ground.

Plants in containers have special watering needs according to the environment, the plant, and the type of pot you choose. You can read more about this topic in Chapter 15, p. 102, in the section on watering.

AIR

It's all around us, so what do we need to know about it? Two things, the first being that some plants are particularly sensitive to air pollution. If that's a problem in your area, buy from a local nursery that knows what survives there.

The second is that dry winds can strip the moisture from a plant quickly and thoroughly, winter or summer. If these are a problem in your area, plant tender, vulnerable specimens in sheltered areas.

Again, remember that roots need air: Dense, compressed soil grows puny plants. Soggy, waterlogged soil rots roots. Even stepping on wet soil can push it down, hardening it. Don't.

Now we've skimmed the surface of the basics. Soil, microclimates, wind effects, and water transport within plants are all subjects you could delve into on a winter night, but with an elementary understanding of the basic ingredients for plant life, you will be able to place plants more confidently, more precisely, and more harmoniously.

On the following page is a checklist you can use to gather details on your own unique environment, the banquet table to which you will invite your plants.

Checklist for Each Bed

Sunlight

Winter
Full sun_____ Dappled sun from overhead trees_____ Which side of house?_____

Spring
Full sun_____ Dappled sun from overhead trees_____ Which side of house?_____

Summer
Full sun_____ Dappled sun from overhead trees_____ Which side of house?_____

Fall
Full sun_____ Dappled sun from overhead trees_____ Which side of house?_____

Temperature

Warmer than normal in summer_____ Gets reflected heat from wall_____
Colder than normal in winter_____ Frost pocket_____

Soil

pH: Acid_____ Neutral_____ Alkaline_____

Texture

Sandy_____ Mixture of sand and finer materials_____ Heavy, high in
clay_____ Mainly clay_____

Soil Color/Organic Matter

Dark (high organic)_____ Medium_____ Light-colored (low organic)_____

Air Spaces

Loose, easy to dig_____ Breaks into clods_____ Compacted_____

Water

Dry in winter_____ Dry in spring_____ Dry in summer_____ Dry in fall_____
Protected from rainfall_____ Wet in winter_____ Wet in spring_____ Wet in
summer_____ Wet in fall_____

Air

Windy_____ Air pollution problem_____

Chapter Three

Trust Your Plants

Nature grows plants well—just look around any field, vacant lot, or woods. Most plants have a place on earth where they grow like weeds, without any help from solicitous gardeners. They can do the same in your garden.

Nature's processes involve a lot of trial and error. You, of course, want to plant once and then sit back on the porch with your feet up. This requires conscious planning based on understanding the factors involved.

What nature wants from your garden is a chance to cover the earth with growing things—nature always tends toward diversity, exuberance, and beauty—in other words, lawn that tends to be a flowery meadow rather than a green carpet.

Nature asks that plants be tough, healthy, and full of energy. Weak, stressed plants attract insects and disease, predators ensuring that the strongest survive. Except for a settling-in period after transplanting, expect the same strength from your garden.

You can't duplicate the wilderness in your yard, but you can create a landscape with the same tenacity. Plant for vigor, toughness, and diversity, then accept a few losses here and there. Respect your plants and their ability to thrive without your help. Consciously set up your garden so you can gradually step out of the picture.

You're going to be matching plants with specific situations—specific patterns of sun, water, and soil. For example, if your spot is sunny and sandy, you should choose shrubs like rock rose *(Cistus)* instead of shade and moisture lovers like rhododendrons. If it's sunny and wet most of the year, try summer-sweet *(Clethra)* or other shrubs native to boggy areas.

Match Your Plants to the Environment

Ten plants for sun and dry soil: smokebush (*Cotinus*), *Ceanothus,* cotoneaster, *Pyracantha,* rosemary, *Rosa rugosa,* yarrow (*Achillea*), bearded iris, blue flax (*Linum perenne*), *Wisteria*

Ten plants for sun and wet soil: ash (*Fraxinus*), willow (*Salix*), sweet gum (*Liquidambar*), pear, red-stem dogwood (*Cornus stolonifera*), *Myrica,* marsh marigold (*Caltha*), *Iris sibirica, Iris pseudacorus, Trollius*

Ten plants for shade and dry soil: *Arbutus unedo,* kinnikinick (*Arctostaphylos uva-ursi*), Oregon grape (*Mahonia*), bishop's hat (*Epimedium*), bear's-breech (*Acanthus*), yellow corydalis (*Corydalis lutea*), *Helleborus,* red valerian (*Centranthus ruber*), lady's mantle (*Alchemilla*), foxglove (*Digitalis*)

Ten plants for shade and wet soil: salal (*Gaultheria shallon*), *Lobelia cardinalis,* mint (*Mentha*), elderberry (*Sambucus*), astilbe, monkey flower (*Mimulus*), piggyback plant (*Tolmiea*), maidenhair fern (*Adiantum*), lingonberry (*Vaccinium vitis-idaea*), goatsbeard (*Aruncus*)

QUESTIONS AND ANSWERS

In Chapter 2, you gathered information on your own yard. Now, how do you get the best information on plants in which you're interested? More importantly, how will you know if a shrub will thrive in your state, your town, or your garden?

Don't be fooled into thinking that impulsively picking up something at the nursery just because it has beautiful flowers is less work than doing a little research. You'll pay for your foolhardiness in extra work for years. Knowledge costs almost nothing.

On the other hand, you don't want to spend hours pouring over books looking for information, unless, of course, this is your way of having fun. What you need is the equivalent of a computer that can give you instant answers to all your questions.

One source is the neighbor down the street with the kind of garden you'd love to have. When asking for advice, consider whether he spends all his free time there, or whether she's fussier than you would be. But if you ask, "What's a sure thing, a plant that will spread happily without much care?" you're likely to get some good ideas.

The next option is asking volunteers at local plant sales. They're likely to be sharing extra plants from their own gardens, the kinds of plants with which you'd have luck, hardy and prolific.

Many states train volunteers with the Extension Service to give advice in Master Gardener clinics. If you have this service available, by all means use it. These people are enthusiastic, knowledgeable gardeners who have been trained to identify problems and help people like yourself get the garden they want.

An invaluable source of help is knowledgeable nursery staff. Don't be afraid to ask questions about their background and experience with plants. Nursery pay is low, so you may find beginners helping out during the spring rush, but anyone who is there for more than a few years is there for the love of it and usually has a store of knowledge to share.

Cultivate an acquaintance with the manager, for instance, of a small, high-quality nursery, and you'll have all the answers you'll ever need,

Choosing the Healthiest Plants

1. Buy from a conscientious, reputable nursery—behind-the-scenes care for plants can make a difference between quick growth and lagging survival.

2. Choose plants with loose, healthy roots. Tight, wound-up roots in containers are difficult to extricate and spread out to start a good root system. Mild root-binding can be cured by cutting off the outer layer or gently tearing it apart.

3. Choose plants with a large root system in proportion to the branches. Big plants in little pots may look like a good deal, but they will often start slowly when planted.

THE LAZY GARDENER • 24

Key Questions to Ask

How much sun or shade does the plant need in my climate?

How much water does it need in my climate?

Does it need quick drainage, or can it take planting in a bog?

Does it need rich soil, or can it survive on a lean diet?

How fast will it grow, and to what height?

How hardy is it? Will it take our coldest winters or freeze out occasionally? Is it vulnerable to late frosts?

How much heat does it need? Does it need extra to flower and fruit?

What disease problems can I expect in my climate? What insect problems?

---

especially if you visit during slow times. You may pay more for plants than you would at a discount store, but healthy plants and good advice more than make up for the cost.

One thing to remember about asking advice: No one knows everything, and everyone is wrong occasionally. Don't expect superhuman traits in anyone, even experts.

As you gather information, start a list of plants that are candidates for a place in your yard—those that fit your garden's wish list as well as your own. If you can see them beforehand in an arboretum or someone else's garden, grown specimens in their full beauty, so much the better.

Or you can work backward, asking the names of particularly attractive trees and shrubs you notice around town. If they're happy in a nearby garden, they will often fit into your own. Still, make sure to ask the above questions so you don't get stuck with a prima donna that demands yearly spraying and weekly irrigation.

Now that you are fully aware of your desires, nature's needs, and even the requirements of the plants themselves, you are ready to create a garden that is satisfying, beautiful, and neglectable.

PART TWO

Planning for Independence

Excellent gardens are rarely chance assortments of plants. Your role as a gardener lies in designing the framework within which trees, shrubs, and flowers can expand, spread and colonize freely into a harmonious picture. Let nature grow the plants with a minimum of interference; you can control the contour of a bed, the curve or directness of a path, the placement of a tree. You can choose a color scheme, the height of shrubs needed for privacy, the presence or absence of daffodils in February. It is your vision that will shape the garden into beauty.

Chapter Four

Designs: Creating the Skeleton

For a garden that looks great right away, carve a strong, coherent structure out of its present chaos. Whether you have an acre of mud, an overgrown city lot, or five acres of woodland, you need to draw some lines.

These may be lines on the ground, defining the shape of a bed. They may also be the vertical lines of large trees. Paths, retaining walls, driftwood, garden sculpture, arbors, and the edges of ponds are all permanent lines defining your garden. They become the bones, the skeleton that gives it form.

Why go to the trouble to create a distinctive form? Because a satisfying design can be filled in with simple, undemanding plants. A dull design may be enlivened by elaborate planting, but at the cost of extra work. Creativity costs nothing. All it asks is a willingness to be bold, playful, and adventurous.

When making a plan, you need to gather facts, requirements, desires, whims, and practicalities—all pieces to assemble in a pleasing pattern. You have your wish list from Chapter 1 and your environmental evaluation from Chapter 2. Now you're going to look at the physical site as sculpture, a place to mold into an attractive container for nature to fill with abundant growth.

BOUNDARIES

What are the absolute necessities, the practicalities you need to include in your design? These could include a path connecting the garage and the back door, a sandbox for the kids, or a place to store garbage cans. List these first.

Next, what existing features must you work around? These include the size and shape of your yard, any trees and shrubs you want to save, and the concrete patio you can't get rid of. Anything you're stuck with becomes a part of the design.

Now think of your property as a room, a geometric shape within which you place other shapes to create a pleasing effect. Some of these shapes are the existing features and the necessities you just identified. Others you may choose more freely.

Beds, paths, rocks, and other inanimate objects are your "furniture," permanent fixtures that can be arranged to give a sense of balance. Set the largest piece, usually the line separating the planting area from the lawn, in place first.

If you wish to draw a diagram of your yard and experiment with various lines on paper, great. It's less work to change penciled shapes than solid ones. Later, you'll want a firm, detailed plan, drawn to scale, to work from as you install the garden in stages over several years.

Beds

Your final step in the preliminary planning stage should always be laying out the line of a bed on the ground using a garden hose. This allows you to see exactly how the bed will integrate with the house and its surroundings.

Keep this line as simple as possible. A lot of in-and-out curves look busy and frivolous; a single sweeping curve commands attention. Geometric shapes, such as squares and rectangles, also have power; place them at unexpected angles to your property line for extra interest.

Using clearly defined geometric outlines is an excellent way to give order to the fertile chaos of self-seeded flowers that lazy gardeners often prefer. Informal, naturalized landscapes are easy-care, but placing them within squares and rectangles gives them much-needed focus.

City gardens, in particular, often need structure to balance abundant growth. Otherwise, informality seems simply untidy.

One of the most attractive city gardens I've ever seen had a jumble of woodland plants, tiny twinflower as a ground cover around rhododendrons, and false lily-of-the-valley spreading into astilbe and goatsbeard, the whole picture neatly framed by a series of square beds. They were like photographs hung on the wall, each one perfectly suited to a small formal space.

Paths

Guides for ramblers, divisions between the cultivated and the wild, or simply routes from one place to another—paths catch the eye. Straight paths are businesslike, formal. Curved ones are casual, often meandering. All protect the lawn or ground cover from wear and tear.

Laying out the lines of a path is easy: For a straight path, use a string stretched between two pegs as a guide; for a curved one, use a garden hose. However, choosing a surface is more complex. Concrete is expensive but stays free of weeds. Less solid surfaces, in my experience, eventually sprout chickweed or grass. Your choice should depend on ease of weeding as well as price and beauty.

Unmortared brick and sharp-edged crushed rock are difficult to weed, while bark is easy, but needs to be renewed occasionally. Small rounded gravel may be a good compromise—it doesn't decay, and won't resist a trowel or knife when needed.

Garden Furniture

The boundary of your yard is one frame; the boundaries of each bed are others. What do you put inside? Plants, of course, but we're making the garden pleasing without them for the moment. Driftwood has possibilities. So does a stump salvaged from freshly cleared land. A bowl of water, a sculpture, a boulder, or a grouping of rocks all can be part of the picture.

Rocks, especially, are ideal skeleton material. Chosen well, their shape and sense of permanence balance transitory annuals and elicit a peacefulness hard to achieve otherwise.

Look for rounded, weathered rocks. You want them to look as if they'd been there a few hundred years, at least. Nothing looks worse than sharp-edged pieces recently blasted out of a hillside, dropped on top of the ground as if by accident. Ask a landscaper to recommend rock-supply companies.

You never see boulders completely exposed in nature—they are almost always half buried, swelling out of the soil. Always place them deep in the ground. Yes, they're expensive and you hate to bury so much of your investment, but properly set boulders are priceless.

If you're on a limited budget, gather the largest flat rocks you can haul and set them together on top of a mound of soil, giving the effect of a broken outcropping of rock. Plant some low, creeping or cascading ground covers in the gaps, and you have a rock garden.

Arbors and ponds are other "furniture" to be placed for interest. Each has a distinctive presence to add to the garden. Arbors add height; ponds add depth. While ponds also add some work in caring for fish and occasional cleaning, they can be less work than caring for a bed the same size. See Chapter 11, p. 77 for construction ideas.

Trees

Trees have strong outlines, vertical silhouettes that expand a design upward. They should be placed and planted as parts of the skeleton, as major design components that need time to grow into their potential.

Try to get a sense of a tree's shape, how broad or narrow its silhouette is; perhaps even sketch a specimen in a neighbor's yard or a park. Visualize it at its mature height (or even put a pole in the ground if that's easier), then choose the right place. Upright, vertical accents, such as the incense cedar (*Calocedrus*) and the Irish yew (*Taxus baccata* 'Stricta'), are best used sparingly; they are like exclamation points. Trees broader than tall, such as the flowering dogwood (*Cornus florida*) and the English oak (*Quercus robur*), give a sense of calmness and serenity, but may only fill out with age. Young trees are often slender. Chapters 9 and 15 discuss how to choose and plant trees in greater detail.

When the skeleton is in place, without a single plant, the garden should feel satisfying and enjoyable. If you can, visit a Japanese garden to view the mastery of this technique. Imagine it without bamboo, ground covers, flowering cherries, and iris. What's left is stark, perhaps, but still beautiful in its balance and interest, each path and rock well placed.

What if your budget doesn't allow the installation of pond, rocks, and arbor all at once? Draw them into your plan, then work them in piece by piece, starting with the most used or visible areas in your yard. Each bed, each piece of the whole, has its own skeleton, its own sculptural possibilities.

One rock and a single piece of driftwood can set the tone for a shady corner near the front door. A large tree with a garden seat beneath may be all that's needed in a back corner.

FOCAL POINTS

When you're content with the bones of the garden, you can start adding shrubs, small trees, and perennials for color, texture, and seasonal interest. Any plant in bloom automatically draws attention; use it to create a focal point, a mini-picture within the garden.

Daffodils, for instance, can be used in a the spring as a central point, perhaps grouped around a shrub that blooms at the same time. Mix in some forget-me-nots or other self-seeding annual, and you'll have compliments coming from all your friends.

A 10-foot bed of foxgloves can make a simple statement. A maple in fall color with chrysanthemums and asters is more complex, requiring more planning. Rather than trying for continuous bloom all over your yard, create a succession of areas of color, each one the focus of attention for a few weeks or months.

For simplicity, stick with three to five easy-care flowers in each grouping, or pair several with a shrub or tree. Or plant a bed with dozens of just one flower, in one color. Elegant simplicity is easier to achieve than complex harmony.

Need ideas? Try brainstorming with a friend. Sometimes I've looked at my own garden in spring and gone into panic. Too many weeds, too many possibilities, too many leftovers from a previous owner.

Easy-Care Flowers

For spring: lily-of-the-valley (*Convallaria*), crocus, star-of-Bethlehem (*Ornithogalum*), Lenten rose (*Helleborus*), grape hyacinth (*Muscari*), love-in-a-mist (*Nigella*), western bleeding-heart (*Dicentra formosa*), evergreen candytuft (*Iberis sempervirens*)

For summer: butterfly bush (*Buddleia*), feverfew (*Chrysanthemum parthenium*), daylily (*Hemerocallis*), harebells (*Campanula rotundifolia*), cornflower (*Centaurea cyanus*), *Cosmos*, baby's-breath (*Gypsophila*), sweet woodruff (*Asperula odorata*), Echinacea, rose campion (*Lychnis coronaria*), bee balm (*Monarda didyma*), evening primrose (*Oenothera*)

For fall: black-eyed Susan (*Rudbeckia*), Japanese anemone (*Anemone japonica*), *Aster × frikartii, Stokesia,* autumn crocus (*Colchicum*), *Cyclamen hederifolium,* dwarf chrysanthemum

For winter: *Camellia sasanqua,* witch hazel (*Hamamelis*), cornelian cherry (*Cornus mas*), winter hazel (*Corylopsis*), *Sarcococca, Viburnum × bodnantense,* winter jasmine (*Jasminum nudiflorum*)

I've learned to call on a friend with an artistic eye to come over and talk me through it. All I really need is a chance to throw out ideas, get back a few new thoughts, put the whole mess in perspective. One other person to look around and say, "Well, you could . . ." is all I need to get me started.

Most people love to be asked for their opinions, given lunch or afternoon tea, and treated like a consultant. If you don't like a suggestion, think about why you don't like it—it may point you in the direction of what you really *do* like.

One book I'd recommend for ideas is *The Natural Garden,* by Ken Druse. Though not exclusively for lazy gardeners, it offers ideas for meadows, woodlands, informal flower gardens, and rock gardens that fit our needs. Sit down with a cup of tea on a winter afternoon and let your dreams take over.

Whatever you do, don't hurry. A design professional might come in and draw a plan immediately, but waiting, observing, and taking the measure of your property yields a harmony impossible to hasten.

Insights will come to you over the months, often while you're standing around, idle, watching butterflies or noticing that the crocus are sprouting. Wait for them, cultivate them. Your design will grow at its own pace.

Chapter Five

Making Choices

The true art of a lazy gardener is in accepting limitations, restrictions, and constraints. The garden center offers a smorgasbord of beauties, luscious garden books tempt with images, and here you are with a budget and only a few hours a month to spare.

No room for fun? On the contrary: All artists work within a frame, within the limits imposed by paint and canvas. Unlimited freedom can actually be more confusing than liberating.

Yes, there are hundreds of beautiful plants available; I fall in love with dozens every time I visit a nursery. But what an impossibility to include them all! You would have a botanical garden, not a yard.

SETTING LIMITS

Simplicity and serenity are the result of choosing limits. How do you do this? Hold your goal in mind. You want, you crave, you truly need an attractive garden that asks little of you but appreciation. That's your frame. Everything else has to fit within that boundary.

Paring the list of possibilities down to manageable size is best done boldly. Your allies are the exercises in chapters 1, 2, and 3. These pinpoint exactly what you want and exactly what your garden has to offer any plant you adopt.

What if your desires outstrip your pocketbook and your free time? Identify your basic needs and see if you can meet them with something smaller. A love of water in the garden could be satisfied by a small fountain or even a large sculptural bowl of water or a birdbath, instead of a stream. Could you be satisfied with several rosebushes instead of a classical rose garden?

Or could you wait a year or two, or five? Some dreams need to be put into form gradually, with small celebrations for each stage completed. Spreading 1,000 dollars over three years looks less daunting than the prospect of paying it out now. Six days of hard labor digging and planting are best similarly dispersed.

Once you identify your needs you can be creative, even sneaky, in meeting them. Need an expensive variety of daylily in just the right shade of pink? Well, you do deserve a reward for that volunteer work you're doing. And your sister would probably help with planting the roses if you promised her cut flowers next year.

If you really want a stream, get a stream. Figure out some way to get whatever your heart desires. This is your space to play, to build, to experiment. If it isn't fun, you won't do it.

To Water or Not to Water. . .

Choices that simplify your gardening life start with a few questions. Which areas will you remember to water, and which you will abandon to exist on nature's supply? If you're in love with dahlias or Japanese irises or geraniums, of course you should have them. Pick a place for them close to the house—and the watering hose. Then choose more drought-resistant plants for the rest of the yard. A rule of thumb is that the farther from the house, the more drought-tolerant the plants should be. Lazy gardeners often have short attention spans, and what's hidden is easily ignored. Draw a line between high-maintenance and low-maintenance areas—a strong, no-nonsense, permanent line.

Designing with Color

Another choice to make that will simplify your designing is a color scheme. Do you like warm or cool colors, or both? Sticking with one set or the other will give your garden a unified, well-designed look with little effort. If you want both, put one color scheme in your backyard and one in the front. Or create separate beds with plenty of blues, purples, and whites between them.

Cool blues and purples look great with hot oranges, golds, and scarlets. Golden yellow belongs with warm tones, and is a good companion for coral pink, while pale lemon yellow can mix with cool pinks and reds that are shaded toward purple.

Often, the color of your house will determine your color scheme. For instance, the purplish-pink blossoms of a flowering plum look stunning next to a gray house because they compliment this cool color, but the same plum would seem slightly ridiculous against tan or yellow. Hold a few pots of annuals up to your walls, then try other colors. What looks really great?

I find intense delight in combinations of plants whose flowers seem to take fire from each other, such as the deepest pink at the center of a rose boosted by the same shade in the tiny flowers of the dianthus beneath, backed by deep purple aconite. A small picture, easy to create, with both simplicity and satisfaction.

Perhaps a painter would know how to mix a cool pink with orange, but I'm content within the parameters of a cool or warm division. There are plenty of other dimensions to fiddle with, including shades of green in the leaves. Leaves variegated with yellow offer a red-orange-gold exploration. Those variegated with silver come to life with a blue-purple-pink continuum.

Texture

Combining a variety of foliage textures can also add excitement to a planting. Try to use at least three different leaf textures in each bed, chosen from the following categories: fine or lacy, bold or broad, linear or swordlike, and medium-textured. A fine-textured juniper ground cover, for instance, can be made more interesting by adding a single clump of yucca or ornamental grass (linear) and three plants of silver king artemesia (*Artemesia albula*) (medium).

Large, bold-leaved plants often like shade. These include foxglove, *Hosta, Bergenia, Helleborus,* and *Acanthus*. These make impressive complements to ferns and azaleas. Don't forget that ground covers can also add textural interest, from the fine-leaved creeping *Veronica repens* and Corsican mint *(Mentha requienii)* to the tongue-shaped leaves of lamb's ears *(Stachys byzantina).*

WEEDING OUT THE CHORES

There will be many others choices to make as you put your garden together, piece by piece. Your first question should always be, "What choice requires the least amount of work?" Then ask, "Which do I like the best?" Masses of heather, for instance, make a lovely ground cover. Other possibilities could include pink-flowered kinnikinick (*Arctostaphylos*) and mats of creeping thyme (*Thymus serpyllum*). However, many varieties of heather, unless sheared annually, lack the density to keep down weed growth while the thyme, though dense, lacks the height. Although you may be fond of heather and thyme, in this case choose the kinnikinick.

It's easy to dismiss a yearly chore like pruning or tying up vines as insignificant, but when you're searching for spare moments between work and packing for a weekend trip, these trifles are going to seem impossible to accomplish.

Raspberries, for instance, are easy to grow in many parts of the country, but tend to become thickets of long canes if neglected. Do you have an out-of-the-way place for unpruned raspberries, or are you going to follow accepted garden practice, taking out the oldest canes and tying the new ones to a frame? It may be a simple chore, but it's easy to put off if you're short of time.

Mindfulness of the work that comes with each purchase should keep you from grabbing thoughtlessly. You can also cut down on impulse spending by raising your standards. Demand that every plant you bring home meet some pretty lofty criteria, such as drought resistance, velvety flowers combined with glossy leaves, or the same shade of pink repeated from ground cover to shrub.

Don't just dash into a nursery. Try different combinations of plants, make trial beds in an uncrowded corner, and play around with colors and textures. Train your sense of design.

Among the thicket of choices to be made, don't forget to plan some time in your garden. This should not be time for chores, but for enjoyment, for pleasure, for delighting in this piece of land you're shaping into beauty.

On a Tight Budget? Sources of Cheap Plants

Friends and neighbors are often glad to share their extras, especially if you help with digging and dividing. If you're extremely patient, take cuttings of their shrubs and trees. It will take a year or two until the cuttings reach the size of a gallon-can nursery specimen.

Local plant sales are spring events of which you can take advantage for inexpensive plants and the virtue of helping out a good cause.

Soon-to-be-bulldozed land is the only place you should collect plants from the wild. Give them lots of care until they replace lost roots.

Ideal gardens are like trees; they can't be hurried. They grow at their own pace, within the frame of your choices. Don't settle for a sloppy fit with your dreams; be choosy, critical, and finicky.

Yes, you will spend more time planning, shopping, and asking for advice. Hard work? Not as hard as weeding. Work is all the replanting you're saving yourself from—the watering, the disaster control, and the disappointments you're avoiding. Choose laziness; choose freedom.

Chapter Six

Walls, Fences, and Other Boundaries

Remember reading *The Secret Garden,* by Frances Hodgson Burnett, when you were small? What made the garden special, a world of its own, were the enclosing walls, the locked door, and the hidden key. The boundaries around the garden became the frame enclosing a living picture, a separate life to enter and enjoy.

Few of us will ever have walled gardens, but take a moment to consider the uses of frames, walls, and boundaries as an aid to creativity, focus, and action. Inside them we are the artists, ripping out stretches of sod, trying swaths of one color, then another. Outside is someone else's domain; we don't have to worry about it.

Your garden needs barriers against roaming dogs and peering neighbors. The choices you made in Chapter 5 need barriers to save them from being run over by impulse buying and frantic weekends.

A wall can be visible and physical or internal and psychological. It can be six feet high and built of brick, or a commitment to spend half an hour a week in the garden sipping coffee. Both protect your private self from invasion.

Even a decision to spend only an hour weeding is still an opening, a potential for creating something wonderful. Viewed from a different angle, it is a decision to spend an hour a week outside, aware of robins and swallows, aware of the grit of soil, aware of earthworms and beetles.

If your gardening time is in danger of being cut away by other chores, throw a garden party next month. Invite your friends or relatives. Motivation will cease to become a problem.

41

CHOOSING THE PERFECT BARRIER

Walls, fences, and hedges are all ways to divide your garden from areas controlled by someone else. In deciding how to enclose your property, the first step is to review your priorities. Do you want a physical barrier against wandering dogs and deer? Do you need to block noise or wind? How much privacy do you need?

If you want to be completely hidden from view, install a solid barrier. For a sense of psychological solitude, a light screen of leaves will suffice. If you'd like to display your garden, put up a low fence to mark your territory.

Fences and Walls

Your choice of materials will be controlled by your purpose and your finances. Walls, solid brick or stone, are expensive but permanent, making excellent support for vines or climbing roses. Fences can be solid or airy, made of wood or wire or even netting from a fishing supply store.

When choosing a material, consider the style of your house and pick one that will be compatible, extending the walls of your home into the garden. Bamboo, for instance, might not be the best choice for a Victorian mansion. Brick and white picket fencing seem more formal than interwoven wood or panels of reed. Rough wood, on the other hand, can complement naturalistic gardens and rustic homes.

Should you install a wall or fence yourself or hire someone to do it for you? It's best to leave brick and stone to the professionals; sturdy, long-lasting construction is well worth the cost. Fences also need firm footings but, with skill and interest, you can do it yourself. Balance cost against the value of another precious resource, your time.

If your material is chosen for thriftiness rather than beauty, you can cover it with a sprawling vine such as winter creeper (*Euonymus*). Stay away from invasive climbers that will trespass on flower beds.

Hedges

Fences and walls have the advantage of being narrow and thin, robbing little space from a small city yard. Hedges, on the other hand, are wider and less formal. Clipping is out of the question. No lazy gardener would saddle himself with a chore like this.

Other Vines for Covering Fences

Akebia, bougainvillea, trumpet vine (*Campsis*), anemone clematis (*Clematis montana*), Japanese hop (*Humulus japonicus*), honeysuckle (*Lonicera*), passionflower (*Passiflora*), Grape (*Vitis*), and *Wisteria*

You could plant some of the narrow evergreens, such as incense cedar (*Calocedrus*) and columnar junipers, such as *Juniperus scopulorum* 'Blue Haven' or *J. chinensis* 'Columnaris', if you want a formal effect. They need no side pruning, though for neatness they do need an occasional topping. Since they're naturally narrow, they must be planted close together, and the expense may equal that of a good fence.

Loose, informal hedges are well suited to lazy gardeners who can spare five or six feet at the perimeter of their yard. You can mix several kinds of shrubs, perhaps flowering at different times, or choose a single one for simplicity. Spiny shrubs such as barberry (*Berberis*) and roses give a soft effect while deterring intruders. Blueberries give you an added bonus of fruit. Dwarf hyssop (*Hyssopus*) can outline an herb garden.

How far apart do you plant shrubs to make a hedge? The standard is half the expected width of the plant when full-grown; five-foot-wide blueberries would be planted two-and-a-half feet apart. You can stretch this a bit if you're willing to wait a few years for solid coverage.

ENTRANCES

Every enclosure needs a gap, an entrance into the private space. Openings can be almost as forbidding as the wall itself, such as a locked gate. Or they can be invitations to come in, visit, and enjoy. Pots of flowers are always welcoming. So is a blooming wisteria arching over a path. Intricate openings such as winding paths create a feeling of transition between the public world and the home, a slowing of pace.

Perhaps it is our barriers, our fences and hedges, that allow us to create arbors and grand entrances to welcome others into our world. Barriers allow us to expand our quirks and peculiar delights into our gardens, creating unique expressions of our personalities. Within their shelter, we can be as lazy as we want to be.

Chapter Seven

Covering Some Ground: Mulches and Ground Covers

are ground is an invitation to those plants we call weeds, such as dandelions, thistles, and crabgrass. They excel in fast growth, covering soil quickly and thoroughly, crowding out less vigorous plants. They have their places—holding sand dunes, perhaps—but your garden isn't one of them.

Consider this hypothesis: Stripped soil is like a wound, an opening in the earth that needs to be covered again. How many places on earth stay barren? Few, and only because of extreme heat, cold, or dryness. Even the forest floor is blanketed with leaves or needles.

Weeds are like scab or scar tissue, quick fixes that allow healing to take place beneath. Healing? Yes. Soil processes are delicate, complex, and vulnerable to the dryness and compaction of bare soil. Beneath leaves or matted plants, these activities can reestablish their full balance.

So to work with nature, we need to respect these processes and bandage wounds with dressings of our own choosing. We get the attractiveness we want; nature gets the soil protection it needs.

There are two ways to do this: plant low perennials or shrubs close together to form a ground cover, or spread a thick layer of bark or other mulch. Both have their advantages and disadvantages.

MULCHES

Mulches are always temporary, needing replenishment as they decay. Mulching adds organic matter to the soil, which is always beneficial, but it also adds extra work. Weed seedlings eventually sprout in any decaying mulch, adding even more work.

On the positive side, mulches reduce evaporation from the soil surface without transpiring water through leaves the way plants would. They are an immediate solution, requiring only shoveling time; can be moved easily if you change your mind; and can be easily weeded if invaded by dandelions or quack grass.

What should you use as a mulch? That depends on what's cheap and easily available in your area. Many types, such as bark and peanut hulls, are by-products of local industries. Ask around for recommendations for your area.

Try to find a mulch that's fine textured, i.e., in roughly half-inch pieces. This size may decay more quickly than two-inch-wide slabs of bark, for instance, but it makes any necessary weeding much easier. Decay rates, of course, vary according to the material and your climate.

Some cautions: Grass clippings, unless used in very thin layers, mat into smelly water-shedding sheets. Mixed with sawdust, however, they make a great mulch. The excess nitrogen of the clippings is balanced by the woody nitrogen-poor sawdust.

Peat moss takes effort to moisten once it dries out and in this state it sheds water, rather than allowing it to pass through into the soil. If you have to use peat, use water with a little soap added to dampen it.

Some mulches, such as pine needles, peat moss, and oak leaves, add acidity to the soil. If you're growing azaleas, this is a benefit. However, if you're mulching spinach or many other vegetables, you'll have to add some ground limestone to counteract it.

How thickly should you apply a mulch? That depends on your material and the plants around which you're applying it. Dense materials can be applied in thinner layers than light ones. Straw, for instance, should be applied in four- to five-inch layers, but you would need only two inches of fine bark.

Be careful when applying mulch around shallow, fibrous rooted plants such as rhododendrons. The roots will smother with more than a half-inch or so of bark.

Black plastic and weed cloth have been used under mulches to keep weeds from growing through them, but I've seen many a garden of weeds happily growing in mulch over plastic. And one of the worst weeding jobs I ever had was picking quack grass roots out of weed cloth. I wouldn't bother with either.

GROUND COVERS

The best use of mulches, in my opinion, is as a temporary covering while a ground-cover plant is filling in. By the time the mulch needs renewing, the ground cover should be thick enough to take over. Eventually, you should be able to forget maintenance on that bed entirely.

Don't pile two or three inches of mulch around a newly placed plant; you'll smother the roots and leaves. Keep it thin—about an inch—right next to the stem, then thicken it to three inches or more between plants. Ground covers that spread by underground stems, however, should be mulched only two inches or less between plants.

In addition to their permanence, the advantages of ground covers may include soil-holding roots, flowers, and berries. An ideal solution? Perhaps.

Disadvantages come up primarily during the immature stage of a ground cover, when it hasn't gotten thick enough to protect itself from invasion by grass and weeds. A thin, young planting of periwinkle (*Vinca minor*) can turn into a solid mat of grass-ridden roots with six months of neglect. The grass is impossible to extricate from the periwinkle, and the only solution is to remove the whole cover and start over.

To act as a good ground cover, a plant should be dense enough to totally shade the ground and high enough to keep down weeds. Six inches should be enough, though very dense plants such as bugleweed (*Ajuga*) can be lower to the ground, while loose ones like cotoneaster 'Lowfast' grow higher. Be warned, however: Once grass gets into the planting, it will shoot up through the tallest mat of leaves.

A ground cover should grow quickly enough to make a solid carpet within a few years, but not so fast that it covers neighboring shrubs. English ivy (*Hedera helix*), common dead nettle (*Lamium maculatum*), and Hall's honeysuckle (*Lonicera japonica* 'Halliana') are all disqualified for this reason. Yes, I know that ivy is attractive, but do you want to cut it out of the trees every year?

Try to find an evergreen ground cover; it can protect the ground all year long. And try to match the watering needs of your ground cover to those of surrounding plants; don't plant bog-loving cranberries in with Mediterranean rosemary and sage.

In its juvenile, high-maintenance stage, any ground cover needs babying. Water, fertilize, and hunt down the smallest weeds. Some covers may even benefit from a yearly shearing back to get them to bush out. Any time you put in now will be repaid by the ease of care needed later.

Obviously, there are limits to how much ground cover you can plant at once. Either you hire someone to do all the work or you install it in small batches. A huge area of ground cover can become one of the worst gardening nightmares possible.

I remember one yard, planted with kinnikinick, that was so overrun with dandelion, sheep's sorrel, and grass that it took me an hour to weed a nine-foot-square patch. Even then, I couldn't get all the weed roots out. A few months later, they probably were all back and growing happily. A mulch would have been a cinch to weed compared to that.

So *never* plant a ground cover unless you can care for it well. Never plant one in ground that has perennial rooted weeds, such as dandelion, quack grass, or dock. (See Chapter 18 for tips on weed removal.) And never plant a ground cover that is too low or too thin-textured to suppress weeds. It will be three times as hard to get unwanted plants out of it as out of bare ground or mulch.

Let's look at some specific types of ground covers. If you want to walk, sit, or play on your ground cover, lawn grass is hard to beat. Yes, it does need watering and mowing, but you can probably get the same satisfaction out of a small circle of grass that your neighbors get out of a huge expanse.

One problem with a smooth green lawn is that nature wants

diversity, abundance—a meadow. Dandelions, clover, thistles, and other weeds seems to be drawn to that green canvas as if they had a role to play. Perhaps an intentionally varied planting would suit your needs and keep them out.

English daisies (*Bellis perennis*) are lovely additions and are low enough to accept constant mowing. Self-heal (*Prunella*), an herb with clusters of purple flowers, often appears on its own. Creeping veronica (*Veronica filiformis*) is considered a serious pest in lawns, but to me its blue flowers and delicate texture add beauty. You could probably start all of these from a neglected lawn for free.

Another ground cover that takes some walking is creeping thyme (*Thymus serpyllum*). Fragrant and colorful in spring, with lavender flowers, it's one of my favorites. Its only drawback is an inability to suppress weeds unless it's quite thick. If you choose creeping thyme, you'll probably have to buckle down and weed frequently until it's mature.

One of my favorite low sprawlers is kinnikinick, or bearberry (*Arctostaphylos uva-ursi*). Native to northern parts of both hemispheres, it has everything: drought tolerance, pink flowers, red berries, and attractive leaves. Treat it well until it fills in, then forget about it.

Pachysandra is a readily available shade-tolerant plant that covers ground quickly. It has small spikes of white flowers and glossy-toothed leaves. Thick enough to hold down weeds, it also tolerates poor soil.

Ground covers have different methods of spreading. Some, such as kinnikinick and the low cotoneasters, are low shrubs with long, sprawling branches that eventually intermingle and become thick. Others send out runners that produce more plants at the ends. Bugleweed (*Ajuga*) is one of the best examples of this type; a single plant becomes 12 plants in a month.

Sun rose (*Helianthemum*), daylilies (*Hemerocallis*), and blue fescue grass (*Festuca ovina glauca*) are simply clumps planted so close together that they close in as they grow. Others, such as English ivy (*Hedera*) and honeysuckle (*Lonicera*), are vines that sprawl and root themselves again and again, sending out shoots from each fresh beginning.

When deciding which ground cover to plant, consider the environmental needs discussed in Chapter 3, how fast it will spread, and the demands it will make on your time. Kinnikinick benefits from shearing once or twice after planting. Heather, however, needs to be cut back

Some Other Independent Ground Covers

Sweet woodruff (*Asperula odorata*)

Bishop's hat (*Epimedium*)

Long-leaf mahonia (*Mahonia nervosa*)

Shore juniper (*Juniperus conferta*)

Sea fig (*Carpobrotus*)

Point Reyes ceanothus (*Ceanothus gloriosus*)

Self-heal (*Prunella vulgaris*)

almost every year. Try to find a ground cover that can be left on its own eventually.

How close together you initially put plants will depend both on your pocketbook and on your impatience. You may opt for either close spacing and quick coverage or wider spacing and waiting.

If you have a slope that needs erosion control, look for the toughest plants you can get with root systems known for density and depth. Soil tends to be poor and thin on hillsides, and the slope makes watering difficult. You'll have to build small basins around each new plant

Tough Ground Covers for Hillsides

Bar Harbor juniper (*Juniperus horizontalis* 'Bar Harbor')

Creeping rosemary (*Rosmarinus officinalis* 'Prostratus')

Winter creeper (*Euonymus fortunei* 'Radicans')

Ice plant (*Mesembryanthemum crystallinum*)

Rock cotoneaster (*Cotoneaster horizontalis*)

Winter jasmine (*Jasminum nudiflorum*)

unless you can get them in just before a rainy season. As always, if you can time planting so nature waters for you, do it.

You may find an expanse of ground cover to be boring. Try a few clumps of tall perennials scattered around. Many, such as iris and Japanese anemones (*Anemone japonica*), will grow through a foot-high mass of leaves without any trouble once established. Plant the perennials before the ground cover gets thick and you'll have a lasting partnership.

Can you allow a ground cover to roam freely through shrubs? Yes, if the shrubs are tall enough to keep their heads clear and the ground cover has no propensity for clambering over and through their branches. The carpet of leaves will keep moisture from evaporating from the soil too rapidly, though they use some of that moisture themselves. Even shallow-rooted rhododendrons seem to benefit from a blanket of undergrowth.

This is truly the function of ground covers: undergrowth, a first layer of plants in your multistoried garden. Don't let the weeds take that position; protect the soil yourself with plants you want.

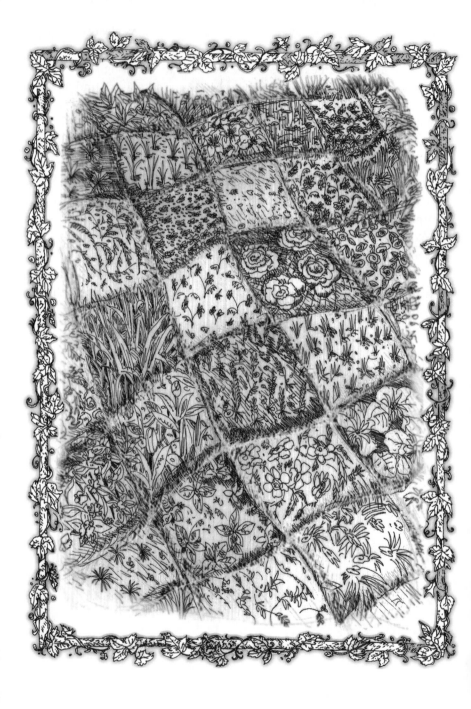

Chapter Eight

Independent Annuals, Perennials, and Bulbs

Is there anyone who really doesn't like flowers? Is there anyone who wouldn't want even a patch of pink or yellow sometime during the summer? Some of us go a bit overboard, trying to pack in as many as possible, but we probably can be forgiven our excesses.

In the back of my mind is an image of a garden filled to overflowing with Siberian iris, Turk's-cap lilies, red roses, purple monkshood, columbine, carpets of harebells, and a thousand other perennials. Take a look at any of the glossy garden books sold and you'll find it somewhere.

The problem is in making the connection between the pictures in my mind and the medium-sized bed in my shady backyard—to say nothing of my budget. Sound familiar? You've probably had the same problem, including the spring insanity attack that drains the checkbook and produces only a scattered touch of color.

What's wrong? Nothing really. You're just in the middle of learning how to garden, not at the triumphant finale. Give yourself time and you'll end up with a garden that's uniquely yours, a combination of plants no one else will ever assemble again.

How? Find out which plants like you and your garden. Find out which ones are so generous with their seedlings that they well deserve the term "weeds." For some reason, plants may sulk in one garden and shine in another, even a similar garden in the same town. Experiment until you find the right partners.

I remember talking to one woman who made a practice of buying one each of a few plants every year. If one did particularly well, the next year she would buy five or ten—an excellent system.

One chore that often comes with growing flowers is deadheading, removing the spent flowers before they set seed. Many plants will bloom longer, trying again and again to reproduce themselves, if withered blooms are removed. If you enjoy this kind of work, go ahead. If you don't, leave them alone. Age, seed pods, and shriveled stems are part of life; why fight the process? You can do a general cleanup in fall, cutting back or pulling out all the dead growth, or even leave the mess to shelter the ground until spring.

ANNUALS

There is something about a mass of a single flower that satisfies. Three foxgloves (*Digitalis*) aren't much to look at, but the 30 feet of white and purple spikes in my backyard last year were a grand show. With foxgloves in your garden, you merely have to scrape the ground bare when they're shedding seeds to have masses of them. They do all the work themselves.

Foxgloves are biennials, making a sturdy plant the first year, then flowering the second. Many choice flowers are annuals, which sprout, flower, and die in a single year. Some of these, called "hardy annuals," will self-seed prolifically around your garden, requiring no more care than the weeds you curse.

One of my favorites is love-in-a-mist (*Nigella*), a feathery foot-high plant with pink, blue, or lavender flowers. 'Miss Jekyll' is a variety with an excellent blue shade. *Cynoglossum* is also blue, with masses of small flowers; it's also called Chinese forget-me-not.

Nasturtiums (*Tropaeolum*) aren't usually considered weeds, but I once cared for a garden where these filled the space under an apple tree each year, popping up regularly in other spaces, too. I raked the soil in fall to cover the seeds, but they did the rest themselves.

Calendulas and forget-me-nots (*Myosotis*) are true gifts to lazy gardeners, filling in any bare soil with carpets of seedlings. They're so prolific that I'd recommend being choosy about which varieties to introduce into your garden. Find the clearest blue forget-me-nots and exactly the shade of calendula you like. Orange is common, but you can find gold and pale primrose yellow varieties, too.

Cornflowers (*Centaurea*) come in shades of pink and purple, but nothing else matches the vivid blue of the original. A 15-foot bed of these mixed with orange California poppies (*Eschscholzia*) will have you on the top-10 list of gardeners in your town.

Sweet alyssum (*Lobularia*) is a good filler almost everywhere, especially in white. It's not as drought tolerant as the previous annuals I've mentioned, but makes pools of bloom in regularly watered beds of shrubs or perennials.

Kenilworth ivy (*Cymbalaria*) is a round-leaved creeper that spills over walls and blankets the ground in shady places. The small violet flowers aren't spectacular, but they add interest. This ivy is perennial in the warmest parts of the country.

Some other hardy annuals to try include baby-blue-eyes (*Nemophila*), Shirley poppies (*Papaver rhoeas*), larkspur (*Delphinium*), and four-o'clocks (*Mirabilis*). If some of these sound unfamiliar, it's because many people know only the tender annuals sold in garden centers. Hardy annuals, adapted to colder climates, give you yards of blossoms for the price of a packet of seeds.

Scatter them over a bare patch of ground in fall or early spring; they'll germinate at the proper time with no care on your part. Be sure you do it before warm, dry weather sets in, however. Lazy gardeners are rarely diligent enough with the watering to get good germination going late in the spring.

One catch: You need to plant self-seeding annuals in ground that is free of perennial weeds such as quack grass. Your plants will crowd out the mild-mannered annuals such as chickweed, but weeds that come up from the roots will have the advantage if there is competition.

Hardy annuals are great, but that doesn't mean you should never buy petunias or marigolds. You just can't get the same show as cheaply.

If you do invest in six-packs of small plants, be sure you get the most from your time and money.

How? One way is to focus your efforts on small, highly visible areas, especially those near the front door. Not only will you savor the fruits of your work every time you pass by, but you'll be more aware of any wilting if you forget to water. You could plant small beds or put your efforts into containers.

A few large pots overflowing with blossoms and set on your porch or deck can be a surrogate flower garden if you can't summon the energy for a whole bed. You can cram lots of bloom into a small space, adding generous portions of trailing plants to suggest overflowing abundance.

Plant the largest containers you can afford in scale with your porch. Small ones dry out faster and tend to look fussy. If you're planting more than a few, it's worth

More Hardy Annuals

Annual candytuft (*Iberis coronaria*), *Clarkia, Cosmos,* annual baby's-breath (*Gypsophila elegans*), sunflower (*Helianthus annuus*), larkspur (*Delphinium ajacis*), tidy-tips (*Layia elegans*), fried eggs (*Limnanthes douglasii*), scarlet flax (*Linum grandiflorum* 'Rubrum'), mignonette

Perennials from Packets

Seed these in fall; many will bloom the first year:

Columbine (*Aquilegia*), bellflower (*Campanula*), yellow corydalis (*Corydalis lutea*), hollyhock (*Alcea*), pink mallow (*Malva alcea fastigiata*), mullein (*Verbascum*), yarrow (*Achillea*), English daisy (*Bellis perennis*), sweet William (*Dianthus barbatus*), cranesbill (*Geranium*), Lenten rose (*Helleborus orientalis*), lupine (*Lupinus*), rose campion (*Lychnis coronaria*), Welsh poppy (*Meconopsis cambrica*), blue-eyed grass (*Sisyrinchium*), meadow rue (*Thalictrum aquilegifolium*), red valerian (*Centranthus ruber*) creating your own soil mix, adding purchased compost and steer manure to the bale of rather bland potting soil you bought.

Use no more than a cup of manure per gallon of mix and enough compost to make the texture crumbly rather than fine.

Containers need frequent watering; you'll have to remind yourself to check regularly to see if they're dry. Don't keep them soggy; when the top inch is dry, soak them again. They need fertilizing also, since the roots are confined. Pelleted fertilizers, though relatively expensive, last the summer on one application. (See p. 113 for more on container gardening.)

For easier care, why not create the same abundance in a small piece of ground? Instead of spreading your box of potted flowers over a whole bed, cram them into a few square feet. Imagine that you're planting a container, putting something tall toward the center and low sprawlers around the edges. Now stand back and congratulate yourself on how fine it looks!

One of the advantages of annuals, either from a nursery or seed grown, is that they have a long season of bloom, often a full summer if spent flowers are clipped. There is, however, another class of flowers, those that usually have shorter blooming periods but make up for this defect by returning year after year in ever-increasing numbers.

PERENNIALS

Perennials are fun and, if you find the ones that like you, ego-satisfying. They die down to the ground each winter, then shoot up again in spring, reappearing spontaneously just when you need a boost. If they're happy, they will crowd out weeds, colonize odd corners, and bless you with masses of flowers.

Their growing points, or crowns, usually form clumps, some tight, some straggly. Each year there are more crowns, and you can often get new plants by dividing a clump into two or three pieces (see p. 108 for details).

What are some of the easiest to grow? That depends on your part of the country, but you'd do well to start off with a selection of these: yarrow (*Achillea*), mountain bluet (*Centaurea montana*), Shasta daisy

(*Chrysanthemum maximum*), sweet William (*Dianthus barbatus*), bleeding-heart (*Dicentra*), daylily (*Hemerocallis*), and Siberian iris (*Iris sibirica*).

One of my favorites is the yellow *Corydalis lutea*, a Mediterranean native with an unmatched propensity to bloom. Masses of its small yellow flowers appear in my garden from February through October. It's also generous with its seedlings as well as drought tolerant—a nearly perfect plant.

Japanese anemone (*Anemone japonica*) is another one of my favorites, with bold leaves and pink or white flowers late in the summer. It spreads well and tolerates dryness. I once had it growing among the roots of an elm, not a perfect situation. It prospered.

Harebells (*Campanula rotundifolia*) deserve to be planted more frequently, especially in neglectable gardens. With tiny bell-like flowers of the typical cool campanula blue, they grow in lawns or rock gardens, seeding ferociously.

Epimedium, or bishop's hat, looks delicate and woodsy, but has a tolerance for dry shade seldom matched. The heart-shaped leaves and sprays of tiny flowers would be welcome in any garden.

Labrador violet (*Viola labradorica*) is another shade-lover with characteristics that make it ideal for lazy gardeners. It's comely and neat, with purple-edged leaves and deep lavender flowers. Its watering needs are minimal, and it sows itself into sheets of color. This is another plant for every garden.

Red valerian (*Centranthus*) stays neat with sun and drought but sprawls otherwise, with pink or white flowers. Each one is tiny, but the clusters show up well in the garden. It's a weed in its habits, but a welcome one to those who appreciate independence.

Baby's-breath (*Gypsophila*) fills in spaces between more upright plants the way florists use it to surround roses with airy elegance. Don't let its delicacy fool you: It can take drought so well that it's naturalized in some near-desert areas. Give it sandy soil to keep it from excess moisture.

One of the mallows, *Malva alcea fastigiosa*, is another delight for neglected gardens. Four feet high, with purplish-pink flowers like small hollyhocks, it needs little water and takes heat well. Plant one and you'll have 20 next year.

Another perennial that acts as a weed is a variety of toadflax (*Linarea purpurea*). Its spikes of tiny purple flowers are welcome almost anywhere, but look especially fine with rose campion (*Lychnis coronaria*). Rose campion has vivid purple-pink flowers and gray leaves, a hint at its tolerance for drought. The flowers are so bright they mix poorly in flower beds, but alone or with a few compatible colors they capture attention.

Staking floppy stems is a boring, often unnecessary chore. One solution is to pile brush over the sprouting crowns of delphinium or tall aster in spring; the stems will grow through the maze of twigs without guidance. Another is to choose plants with stout stems, such as foxglove, *Anemone japonica*, monkshood (*Aconitum*), hollyhock, meadow rue (*Thalictrum*), and mallow (*Malva*).

If you consider yourself afflicted with a boggy area, check out some of the perennials that prefer wet soil. *Iris pseudacorus* is a rapidly spreading yellow-flowered beauty. Marsh marigold (*Caltha palustris*) is likewise golden, but with round leaves and a lower habit. Globeflower (*Trollius*) blooms yellow to orange and looks somewhat like a large, half-open buttercup. You can experiment with some of the candelabra-type primroses such as the purple, pink, or white *Primula japonica*. For bold leaves, if you have space, plant butterbur (*Petasites*) with spikes of purple flowers or umbrella plant (*Peltiphyllum*) with white sprays of flowers and leaves up to two feet across. Other plants to try are: obedient plant (*Physostegia*) with spikes of pink, tubular flowers, spiderwort (*Tradescantia*) with three-petaled white, blue, or purple flowers, and cardinal flower (*Lobelia cardinalis*), an attention-getter with vivid scarlet blossoms.

There are, of course, many more excellent perennials available. Ask around for local favorites, since what grows profusely in one place may be a difficult-to-grow specialty a few hundred miles away.

You may even find a neighbor who is happy to offer you extra plants. I remember walking by someone's house and admiring the lamb's ears. The woman offered me some, saying, "God grows 'em; I just spread 'em around."

Or you can pick up advice and inexpensive plants at local garden sales to benefit hospitals or other charities. Many of these come out of the gardens of the volunteers selling them, most of whom will be happy to share their knowledge. Often, you'll find samples of exceptionally prolific plants that grow almost anywhere.

Others spread by underground stems, and here you need to strike a balance between spreading and invading. I planted one coltsfoot (*Tussilago*) last year and have it covering 40 square feet this year. As much as I like its broad leaves and carefree habit, I think I'll restrict it to the back of the yard from now on.

Mints can be overwhelming, as can comfrey (*Symphytum*) and bluebells (*Endymion*). What about a bed devoted only to pushy plants like these? Let them fight it out among themselves; you just sit back and enjoy.

Some perennials that make thick clumps without quickly overrunning their neighbors include Japanese anemone, sweet woodruff (*Galium odoratum*), mountain bluet (*Centaurea montana*), lamb's ears (*Stachys byzantina*), and Shasta daisies (*Chrysanthemum maximum*). You can rapidly increase your stock of these by division.

BULBS

Perennials are fun, but bulbs are magic. Dry, rootless brown shapes dropped into the ground in fall, they seem to disappear until suddenly a bud or a leaf surfaces. Who can resist them?

Some of a lazy gardener's best friends are bulbs. They plant easily, return yearly, and, with some exceptions, spread with abandon. For many, dry summers are their time-out, a dormant period they survive by retreating into bulb form. Water sparsely, if at all, unless you know they need moisture to survive.

Take a few moments to stir some bone meal into the soil below the bulb, perhaps a teaspoon for each one. High in phosphorous, this fertilizer promotes root and bulb growth, helping these plants renew themselves year after year.

Crocuses are common and easy, good for beginning gardeners. My favorites are the small wild types such as *Crocus tomasinianus*, a master at seeding itself around. Plant among perennials or in a low, dense ground cover.

Daffodils (*Narcissus*), of course, are classics, but you want the ones that will extend their territory each year. Pick the common, less expensive varieties, those that say "for naturalizing." These should be tough and carefree.

Some of my particular favorites include *Cyclamen, Brodiaea, Allium, Alstroemeria, Colchicum,* and star-of-Bethlehem (*Ornithogalum umbellatum*), all drought-tolerant. If you don't know them, find pictures in bulb catalogs or try a few as an experiment. Check hardiness for your area before you plant, though.

Because of high nutrient needs, tulips often get smaller in size and fewer in number rather than increasing each year, so skip them unless you're willing to replant frequently. Other bulbs to avoid, unless they're favorites you're willing to work for, are those not hardy in your area. You don't need the work of digging in fall and replanting in spring.

Again, if you come across a plant that seems to do well in your garden, don't be afraid to plant lots of it. Most yards look too spotty rather than monotonous. One year I scattered seeds of Welsh poppies (*Meconopsis cambrica*) in *Ajuga* and had a hundred of them in bloom the next year. Another time I seeded *Cynoglossum* in front of white-flowered *Cistus* shrub, making a 20-foot swath of blue. Both were more striking than any melange of perennials would have been.

As you can see, a passion for flowers can be satisfied without breaking your back or your bank account. Go for simplicity, using masses of a few good-natured flowers for maximum impact. Relax and let them do the work.

Chapter Nine

Shrubs and Trees: The Flesh on the Bones

Easy-care woody plants, the ones you choose because they suit conditions in your garden, add height, softness, and sometimes color. No matter how interesting the basic design, your garden would seem stark and flat without shrubs and trees.

However, careful planning is essential; five years' growth is hard to replace if you've made a mistake. A viburnum in a one-gallon can usually cost less than 10 dollars. The same viburnum with another year's growth, now in a five-gallon can, will cost you 30 dollars or more. A few more years and it would cost 200 dollars to move a mature specimen in.

The largest trees were placed as part of your bare-bones design in Chapter 4, but small ones can give height to clusters of bushes along fences and property lines. Take a look at your plan, then at your yard. Visualize shapes and contours, heights and widths, all to clothe the austerity you find now.

Perhaps a sketch would help you see the picture more clearly, or borrowing prunings off a neighbor's tree and sticking them in the ground. In a pinch, you can even rent some trees and large shrubs from a nursery for a day, setting them here and there, experimenting.

The purpose of this exercise is to get a clear picture of the outlines you'd like to create. How high, how wide, and how straight or curving a silhouette do you want? Do you need some openness here, perhaps a small, graceful tree, and density over there? This is your landscape; you set the stage.

What other purposes do you want your shrubs to serve? Most yards haven't room for anything that doesn't do double duty in some way. Flowers are certainly high on most people's wish list; choose a tree or shrub with attractive form and foliage when out of bloom. Forsythia, for instance, charms with extra-early blossoms but looks dowdy and graceless the rest of the year.

Spiny plants like barberry *(Berberis), Pyracantha,* and roses make excellent barriers. Other shrubs have dense root systems that stabilize steep banks. Make sure you get all the practical work you need, as well as the frivolity you enjoy. Trees and shrubs can handle both.

Shrubs with Dense, Strong Root Systems

Abelia, kinnikinick (*Arctostaphylos uva-ursi*), flowering quince (*Chaenomeles*), rock rose (*Cistus*), silverberry (*Elaeagnus*), winter jasmine (*Jasminum nudiflorum*), ground-cover types of juniper (*Juniperus*), creeping mahonia (*Mahonia repens*), *Pyracantha* 'Santa Cruz', rugosa rose (*Rosa rugosa*), rosemary (*Rosmarinus*), lavender cotton (*Santolina*)

Do you notice the similarity to our previous planning sessions? First, get clear about what you want and what you need, then move into making choices. Work from broad decisions down to buying specific plants. Make sure you get maximum satisfaction from your design.

PLANNING FOR GROWTH

How do you narrow down plant possibilities? Your outline sketches will give you mature heights to look for, usually given as a range, such as five to eight feet. This is a height you can expect in normal garden soil under average conditions in about 10 years. Ten years? But you want a lush garden in two or three at the most!

The temptation here is to choose something fast-growing to get the effect you need as quickly as possible. Sure, you could have something substantial in your yard in a few years. The problem is that five years later you'd have a nightmare of too-tall, overcrowded plants. For example, the deodar cedar (*Cedrus deodara*)—which grows to 80 feet tall with a 40-foot canopy—is often planted with distastrous results in 20×20-foot front yards by people who want a tree in two years. And I've seen rock rose (*Cistus*) placed in narrow beds unable to hold its 5×5-foot shape. The result? A yearly battle to prune it down to knee-height.

Of course, if you're planning on moving in five years, you can plant fast-growing trees or shrubs and then duck out of the consequences. Or you could take half of them out and give them away or donate them to charity. Or you could cut them back twice a year.

You could also plant a fast-growing tree next to the slow-growing one you intend to have permanently and take out the first one in five or 10 years. Or you might plant things closer together than recommended, then transplant some of them to a new bed you'll be making in a few years.

You can certainly spend the money to buy a fairly substantial tree to start off with, which might be worthwhile if it's the cornerstone of your design. Just remember that growth continues throughout a tree or shrub's life. If a book says it's a 15- to 20-foot tree and you buy one 10 feet high, it may be 25 feet in 10 years.

One well-kept secret is the fact that many large shrubs can be pruned up and thinned out to make quite respectable small trees. Simply remove all but one main stem, then prune off the smallest branches from that new trunk. If you need a small tree to take center stage fairly quickly, consider this option.

FINDING THE PERFECT PLANT

So now you have desired heights, a variety of purposes you want your purchases to serve, a firm grasp of the conditions you have to give them (see Chapter 2), and a total blank on specific plants. What do you do?

You could study a plant encyclopedia or consult lists entitled "Shrubs (or Perennials or Trees) for Sun or Shade" in other books. One problem with these methods is that many shrubs listed may not be commonly available. Another is that the information isn't local and specific. Take your wish list to a large nursery and see if they can help you find a fit.

Nurseries exist to sell plants. Good nurseries realize that the best way to do this is to help customers get exactly what they need, which means having trained professionals to give advice. A good nursery also takes better care of its stock than your average bargain lot. Yes, they

Fast-Growing Fillers

Here are some better ideas for fillers while you're waiting. Plant tall annuals, such as sunflowers, in the spaces. You can also try: *Angelica,* coneflower (*Rudbeckia*), *Cosmos,* foxgloves (*Digitalis*), evening primrose (*Oenothera*), flowering tobacco (*Nicotiana*), larkspur (*Delphinium*), or spider flower (*Cleome*).

Perennials may not get as tall or bushy the first year, but here are some to plant for height: monkshood (*Aconitum*), many types of aster, snakeroot (*Cimicifuga*), sneezeweed (*Helenium*), mallow (*Malva*), plume poppy (*Maclaya*), meadow-rue (*Thalictrum*), valerian (*Valeriana*), and hollyhock (*Alcea*).

may be more expensive, but you'll get more in the long run buying at a competent nursery than trying for bargains.

With all your planning you can be specific about what you need, and a nursery professional can find the best fit with the plants he or she knows. Be prepared, however, for some priority juggling before you buy.

For instance, perhaps you've decided you want a tree 30 feet high that will have nice fall color, have flowers in spring, and grow in the bog you have at the end of your property. Well, that's a pretty tall order. Very few trees with spring color, such as cherries and crab apples, will grow in wet soil. A pear tree would take some extra water in the soil but wouldn't get as tall as you want. An empress tree (*Paulownia*) would grow fast and have beautiful flowers, but would be 50 feet tall before you know it. What about sour-gum (*Nyssa sylvatica*)? It doesn't have flowers, but the fall color is gorgeous. As you can see, narrowing the possibilities down to one can be difficult. You may have to give up one thing you wanted to get others, so decide what's most important. Is it flowers or fall color? Is it height or fruit?

With trees, in particular, ask about potential pest and disease problems. You'll be investing years in a tree before full growth, and you don't want your time to go down the drain. Also ask if your possibility has greedy roots that would clog drains and empty the soil of water and nutrients. Willows are notorious villains; avoid them if you don't have an acre of moist soil for roots to spread.

If you want fruit, again be sure to ask for disease resistance. Plums tend to be carefree; other fruit trees may do fine depending on your part of the country. Conversations with neighbors and nursery professionals can be illuminating.

IT'S ALL IN THE ROOTS

When it's time to buy, what should you look for in nursery stock? Healthy green color, generous top growth that is in proportion to the container (overly root-bound plants are hard to get going in the ground), a strong root system if bare-root, and a symmetrical branching pattern.

When you buy a tree or shrub, the roots will be protected in one of three ways. First, with what is known as bare-root stock, moist sawdust (or another material) is piled over the roots or packed around them. It's the least expensive method, providing a clear view of the root system, but must be sold in early spring before leaves appear. Don't buy it later.

Second, with balled and burlapped stock, a mass of soil containing the roots has cloth wrapped around it to protect it and hold it together. The soil is usually heavy and firm—an asset in keeping the root ball intact, but liable to dry out more quickly than your own. Water regularly until the roots are well established.

Third, with container stock, a solid wall of plastic surrounds the root ball, extending above it to provide a watering well. Plants in containers are often expensive, but they transplant well with no stress on roots.

Often, your choice will be available in only one of these forms, though bare-root stock is often planted in containers just before it leafs out. So, you've just bought a maple, or three forsythias, or 12 heathers. What next? Consult Chapter 15 for planting instructions and ready yourself for some work. No matter how tempted you are to shirk, don't skimp on the size of the planting hole; loosening the soil gives roots a head start. Water with a rooting solution, stand back, and admire.

Does this involve more work than planting annuals? Of course, but these mainstays of gardening give you far more than they take. You'll be admiring them for years.

Chapter Ten

Do You Really Want Vegetables?

hy would you step into the esoteric world of vegetable growing? Because you're a gourmet searching for the best flavor? Or because you're curious and want to try growing your own tomatoes just once?

Walk in with your eyes open. Growing food is where gardening gets serious. With few exceptions, vegetables ask for more watering, weeding, fertilizing, soil preparation, and pest control than many other plants. And don't forget the time spent harvesting.

That said, I have to admit that there are few more rewarding experiences than eating food out of your own garden. You've watched the leaves get bigger, the stems get longer. You've watched the flowers open and set fruit. Now you pick your first tomato and eat it, warm and fragrant, while you stand in the sun, barefoot.

Idyllic? Yes, but that's what gardens are for. If your dreams include vegetables, let's look at ways to cut down on the work.

Plants we grow for food vary in their needs, just as other plants do. Most vegetables, however, have been bred for flavor rather than toughness, for normal garden conditions rather than lazy gardening. This gives them a penchant for rich soil and plenty of water.

There are exceptions. Jerusalem artichokes are notorious weeds, spreading their small tubers into square yards of almost any soil. Kale and parsnips can seed around indiscriminately if allowed. Even potatoes can form self-renewing populations from unharvested tubers.

Herbs, on the other hand, tend to be rugged and self-reliant, perhaps because they've been grown for centuries by people too busy with other chores to pamper them. Our ancestors, after all, were usually more concerned with survival than flavor; many of our culinary herbs were first brought into gardens for their medicinal virtues.

THINK SMALL

Ah, but the problem is you want tomatoes, or peas, or lettuce, not strange-tasting Jerusalem artichokes! My advice to you, then, is to start small. Try one tomato plant, a six-pack of lettuce seedlings tucked in among the flowers, or even a circle of dwarf peas behind the petunias. Mix them with your high-maintenance plantings, if you can.

Treat this as a project for the kid in you. Mix the zucchini with petunias, plant in curves, and hire someone to water. Treat the necessary digging and soil preparation as college-level mud-pie making, as a way to get your aggression out, as a challenge to your strength.

Put vegetables near the watering hose, to minimize hauling it back and forth, and near the back door, where you'll see them frequently. Not only must you be aware of watering needs, but harvesting demands almost daily awareness of what's ripe and what isn't.

Perhaps a full vegetable bed is in your future. Perhaps it would end up half full of weeds. Early spring enthusiasm builds far more veggie gardens than ever make it through the summer; don't let your bucolic images trick you into planting more than you can care for.

What are some good vegetables for small areas? Carrots and radishes, sown in small patches rather than rows. Bush beans and peas. One or two small varieties of tomatoes. Broccoli and greens.

Green onions or scallions can be started from the rooted ends of store-bought bunches. Simply put them in water until the roots are longer, plant, and wait until new leaves appear.

Lettuce and other leafy vegetables are easy to mix with flowers and take more shade than many others. In general, they need a richer soil than plants grown for their fruit, such as tomatoes; give them whatever they need. You can add manure or compost to the soil, then sprinkle with liquid fertilizer occasionally. Try the high-maintenance routine this year, then decide if it was worth the trouble.

Other vegetables have their own wish list. Potatoes like acidic soil that is light and sandy; spinach needs neutral soil that is light with not much clay; celery needs rich, somewhat acid and highly organic soil. Peas can be planted when the soil is cool; corn sulks unless the soil is warm.

Obviously, you can't please them all. Know your own garden and plant those vegetables that will like what they find there. This may take a little experimentation, a willingness to try a few of something, then plant more next year if you're successful. Don't feel guilty over your failures; even expert gardeners lose a few battles occasionally.

You can avoid many failures by seeking out good local advice, an essential when you start growing vegetables. Books written for a nation-wide audience talk in generalities; the local organic gardening organization focuses on exactly what grows well in your town. They'll tell you what pests and diseases to look out for, recommend the easiest types of vegetables to grow, and give you lots of smiles and pats on the back.

Try to resist any encouragement to delve into vegetable gardening too deeply, however. Good-hearted enthusiasm can be infectious, but where do vegetables fit in your priorities? Are you starting anything that is going to keep from taking the kids camping? Can you have a marriage and a vegetable garden? If you're single, you have friends and other projects to cultivate.

You can, of course, involve friends or family in the project, making your time serve double duty. Food suddenly appearing on plants fascinates kids; you may be able to use your children as apprentice weeders and waterers. Digging together could make a marriage stronger. You know your family; make your own decisions.

CREATIVE EDIBLE GARDENING

Again, we come to the process of setting barriers, boundaries to keep your time in your own hands. How tough are you going to be? Each small plot of high-maintenance garden has a cost in time and energy. Do you want to pay it?

Gourmet Weeds

Let's get adventurous now and look at some radical ways to put food in your garden. Weeds are certainly durable and independent. You could sow improved varieties of dandelion and purslane. Or corn salad, a small green that seeds wildly, with abandon.

Asparagus grows as a weed in some arid areas, yielding only thin spears but caring for itself and flourishing. Could you disobey all traditional gardening wisdom and treat it as a dry-lander?

Artichokes, also, are said to need plenty of water, though I once saw an energetic specimen growing in a hot dry Italian backyard. More opportunity for experimentation.

You probably have smooth chickweed in your garden, a green with a pleasant taste, easily mixed with salads. Shepherd's purse is peppery, a bit like mustard. Sheep sorrel, too invasive to plant but sometimes present despite your best efforts, adds a lemony tang to soups. What about an intentional weed bed?

Gone to Seed

Kale and broccoli could join the dandelions, if you neglect a few plants and let them seed. They certainly would not confine themselves to neat rows, but you could live with a few coming up in odd corners, couldn't you? Try some other greens, such as lettuce, arugula, and radicchio, or some of the mustards.

As you can see, some of your "failures," such as the cauliflower and brussels sprouts bolted and gone to seed, can be turned to good use, with a little disdain for neatness. Rotted tomatoes and squash you forgot to harvest tend to produce lush plants next year. Even peas left on the vines can sprout unexpectedly the following spring if cleanup isn't too thorough. After all, the business of seeds is to sprout.

Wild Things

Or, working in another direction, introduce some wildlings into your garden. Miner's lettuce (*Montia*), a native used in salads, has small leaves that can quickly carpet shady areas, places not often used for vegetable growing.

Wild food books list numerous plants you could invite into your garden. Salsify, prickly pear, orach, and even nettles provide food for little work. Fireweed (*Epilobium angustifolium*) has tender new shoots to offer, and evening primrose (*Oenothera*) has roots to steam or add to stews. Perhaps you can select the best-tasting individuals to propagate.

Some of these were originally used in Europe as potherbs, miscellaneous cultivated or wild foodstuffs. You might find others available from local herb growers, such as French sorrel, marsh mallow (*Althaea officinalis*), and good King Henry (*Chenopodium bonus-henricus*).

Herbs

Herbs themselves are often carefree additions to the garden. Many, such as rosemary, thyme, oregano, and sage, are native to the Mediterranean and therefore do well with little water. Others, such as parsley and chives, combine well with flowers and can take shade.

Numerous varieties of mint are well known for their ability to cover ground rapidly, so much so that you may want to confine them within pots. I prefer to foster their generous disposition and plant them with *Ajuga* and Welsh poppies (*Meconopsis cambrica*) as a ground cover for dry shade.

Friend or Foe?

A word about pest control in the vegetable garden: Humans have some primal emotion that is triggered by competition for food. We don't even think. It's "Smash him or I'll starve." Raccoons may be cute from a distance, but when they ravage our corn we're ready to get out the shotgun.

Stop and reflect for a moment. Are you really in need of this food? Can you choose something else? Are you being given feedback from nature indicating this plant is too weak, too stressed, or in the wrong place?

In my garden, slugs are prime competitors for delicate, luscious treats like fresh lettuce. I have better success growing these vegetables in containers, simply removing them from the battlefield. Planting extra and letting the strongest survive works also. As always, strategy works better than head-on confrontation.

Personally, I feel that there are a lot of organic farmers out there who could use our help. We'd feel virtuous in supporting them, and they'd get the money. We would have some extra time, and they would have customers. Balancing, weighing, and deciding are, as always, hard work.

Again, if you're going to grow a vegetable, any kind of vegetable, think small!

Chapter Eleven

Welcoming Wildlife

Gardening for the animals adds a new dimension to your home, turning it into a haven for species both beautiful and curious. From the sound of woodpeckers exploring a dead branch to finding salamanders at the edge of your pond, wildlife gardening can provide new experiences in your own yard.

You can help some species of birds and animals build their populations. You can relish the satisfaction of nuthatches nesting in your trees. You can watch butterflies "puddling," or congregating at moist ground.

There is little extra work involved in wildlife gardening. Lazy gardeners often start off a few steps ahead when it comes to attracting wildlife; we tend toward untidiness and a certain live-and-let-live attitude that allows us to coexist peacefully with wild things.

Our lawn is a delight to seed-eating birds, if a horror to the neighbors. The pile of apple tree prunings left by the back fence already shelters wrens, beneficial insects, and salamanders. Somehow, laziness and wildlife just seem to fit together easily.

And there are excellent excuses for cultivating laziness in planting for wildlife, including reasons to leave part of the lawn completely unmown, put in native plants that take less care, abandon the pesticides, and leave dead flowers to go to seed.

The challenge is in the planning stage, in finding ways to fit everyone's needs together harmoniously. The key is in striking a balance between what you need in your garden and what wild animals need.

Up to this point in the book, we've looked at your own needs, desires, and priorities. Now look at your garden from the point of view of a bird or a butterfly or a salamander. What would you need to be happy in this place if you ate seeds or bugs or drank nectar?

Wild animals have the same needs you do: food, water, protection, and room to roam. If they can find any or all of these in your garden, they'll show up and stay around. The more they find what they need, the more often they'll come, perhaps nesting and becoming permanent settlers.

Of course, if you live 20 miles from the nearest frog, with roads in between, your chances of having frogs croaking in your pond are slim. You'd be surprised, however, at the adaptability of many species. Individuals show up in odd places—a fox in the middle of a city, or a salamander under freeway debris.

WHAT'S ON THE MENU?

Food can be seeds from a bird feeder (not too lazy, since the feeder needs to be filled regularly) or seeds and berries produced on your own plants. It can be insects or flower nectar, or even nettles to feed caterpillars of the red admiral butterfly.

Cater to something as mundane as a caterpillar? Why not? Though the butterfly stage has all the glory, both larva and adult need feeding, often requiring quite different plants. Poplars, willows, cherries, and other trees and shrubs host many larval butterflies, though some prefer bleeding heart, wild carrot, or clover.

Adults are less choosy, going for many nectar-bearing flowers. They tend to be attracted to large masses of a single flower, especially those that are flat enough to rest on, daisies and thistles being favorites.

How do you know what to serve at your garden smorgasbord? Your state Department of Wildlife may be helpful, and the local Audubon Society is a good source for information on more than birds. Ask around at plant sales for someone whose hobby is enticing wildlife into his or her garden.

You'll want to start with the most common species, the visitors you can count on right away. Don't plant something that provides food for a rare butterfly until you know such butterflies are in your neighborhood. Don't set yourself up for disappointment. Commoners are exciting now; invite the nobility in later.

In general, native plants will be the best bet for planting, though some introduced shrubs and weeds are favorites. There are subtle bonds between members of the same ecosystem. Rufous hummingbirds, for instance, arrive in my area at the same time the red-flowering currants (*Ribes sanguineum*) bloom, providing them with a month's supply of food.

PUDDLES AND PONDS

Water in your garden can be as simple as a faucet dripping into a puddle or as elaborate as an artificial stream. Birdbaths need to be cleaned out occasionally, a chore that lazy gardeners usually put off too long.

Is there a naturally wet area that can be turned into a pond? Low ground can be boggy, a challenge for traditional gardening. If you look at it from the view point of frogs and water plants, you'll find your challenge turning into an asset.

If there is no wet area for a pond, you can build one yourself. Small ponds with gently sloping sides are excellent draws for all kinds of wildlife and can be made cheaply using bentonite clay bought at a building supply store.

Dig out your pond in whatever shape you choose, four or five inches deeper than you want it to end up. The finished depth should be at least a foot and a half at the deepest point so your pond can achieve the proper balance of decay and plant and fish growth. Lay some sheets of plastic down for extra leak protection. Then mix clay with some of the extra soil, cover the plastic completely with about four or five inches' worth of the combination, and tamp down. You can also use special pond liners of heavy plastic, which are expensive but permanent. If you do, make sure the sides are buried under soil or stones; nothing looks more artificial than plastic edges. If you buy a ready-made plastic form, be sure to provide some access across the steep sides, such as a piece of driftwood or a pile of stones.

When you're finished, fill the pond and add water plants and fish. You don't have to spend extra for fancy carp; tiny feeder goldfish bought at a fish store for pennies will do fine for keeping down mosquito larvae and will eventually become large and showy.

Aquatic plants assist in balancing your pond, using up nutrients produced by decay that might otherwise nourish excess algae growth. Try for about two-thirds coverage of the water by plants during summer.

If your pond is likely to freeze over in winter, consider purchasing the type of heater farmers use for stock troughs: a round floating heating coil using minimal electricity. Most fish can survive the cold, but need to have some open water to release gases produced by decay.

PRESERVATION

Now that you've taken care of food and water, immediate needs for wildlife, think about long-term necessities. Just as you need walls and a roof to keep out the weather, animals need places to hide and raise their young. Protection may be an old dead tree to a woodpecker, or a pile of brush to a snake. Trees and shrubs, rock piles and rock walls, and hollow logs and bat houses all provide shelter from hungry predators and freezing winds.

Pay particular attention to providing areas that are safe from roaming house cats, such as thickets of thorny bushes. Cats quickly destroy ground-nesting birds and other wildlife if not discouraged.

While you're thinking about protection, throw out all your pesticides, even the less toxic varieties. Butterflies, in particular, are especially sensitive to chemicals. Even the commonly used nontoxic biological control *Bacillus thuringinensis* should be sworn off, since its caterpillar-destroying properties aren't limited to killing moths and other destructive kinds.

Meadows and Hedgerows

Shelter, nesting sites, and food can be combined into one as a hedgerow. A closely planted collection of trees, shrubs, vines, and whatever else strikes your fancy, hedgerows are also dense barriers against noise and staring eyes. Give them eight to 10 feet to spread, and be sure to include favorite seed, nut, and berry shrubs.

The ideal complement to your hedgerow is a meadow of flowers maturing into nutritious seeds, a field rich with insects attracting swallows and other birds. Not your average lawn, is it?

One solution is to mow part of the lawn and leave the rest to go to wilderness, cutting it back once in spring and fall. If you make an attractive curve at the border between the two areas and mow a path or two through your meadow, the untidiness will look well designed and purposeful.

Another solution is to plant special areas of wildflowers that will reseed for next year. Beware of cheap mixes that call themselves "Wildflower Meadows." Most of the seeds are from common garden annuals—wild in Europe, perhaps, but nothing to bother with here. Try to get seeds of local wildflowers, creating your own mix for your climate and ecological region.

Woodlands conceal a multitude of wildlife possibilities. Fifty-foot firs or maples, 20-foot crab apples, eight-foot salmonberries, and a carpet of ferns all provide different kinds of shelter and food for birds and other animals. A diversity of layers brings the greatest diversity of species.

The edges where meadow and forest meet are often the richest habitats, providing the greatest variety of food and shelter. If you can, intensify these borders by using meandering lines and half-hidden nooks tucked back from view. Birds, in particular, will wander back and forth across the border to find what they need.

Get Local Advice

The kinds of birds, butterflies, and other wildlife that live near your home may be different from those near a town a hundred miles away and have little in common with those on the other side of the country. Before buying expensive books oriented toward attracting animals that may not live nearby, consult your trusty county extension service, state Department of Wildlife, and local Audubon chapter.

Yards can be registered as wildlife sanctuaries—so can neighborhoods. Share what you learn with your neighbors; you may be surprised at the enthusiasm you spark.

Chapter Twelve

Your Garden as a Sacred Space

Superficiality isn't rewarding. The more meaning we find in daily life, the more satisfaction we'll get out of it. So how can we tie our gardens into the web of a deeper life?

First, decide what's most important to you, what touches the center of your soul. Is it an alpine meadow, high mass in a church, a Zen meditation, or a wild dance under a full moon? Whatever your most significant moments, you can find an object, a plant, or a shape to symbolize them and place it in your garden.

One person might have a statue of St. Francis, another might place a rock from a favorite mountain next to a pine tree, and a third might hang from the gatepost the head of the "Green Man," a European mythical figure that sprouts leaves and tendrils. Someone might create an altar out of stones, moss, and crystals. Another might find that a hand-made pottery bowl filled with water reminds him of lakes and streams and the sea.

The frame, the boundary, can be set with small stones or with walls and fences and placed with the intention of creating a space of blessing within. This stage is important. It creates a place within which something special and unique can happen. Without the forming of a sacred place, there is no gathering of potential. Without barriers, this potential dissipates.

SHAPES AND SYMBOLS

You can use shapes with universal and personal meaning as boundaries for beds and other spaces. Circles, squares, and triangles all have archetypal significance in some manner. You probably have your own favorite shapes; you can read up on their meaning.

Spirals, yin-yang symbols, triskeles (similar to the yin-yang but with three divisions), and mandalas are all patterns within a circle that can be traced inside beds or courtyards. Herb gardens, in particular, lend themselves to planting in such shapes, though why not use a strawberry bed or a lawn? Lines can be traced in grass using bricks or stones set well below a mower's blades.

In using symbols like these, we invite our deeper selves to enter our garden. The Japanese are masters of the of symbolic garden. The art of suggesting the mountains with a few well-placed rocks, the city harbor with a straight edge to a pond, the cultivated land with a few cherry trees, has been explored and refined over centuries. These objects become the words in a language which transforms a walk through a garden into a journey from wilderness to civilization, a tiny city lot into the emodiment of a bamboo grove.

Just as all sorts of things can turn up as dream symbols, all sorts of objects can connect us with our gardens. A single glass Christmas ball hung on a tree could represent the earth. A wreath of flowers you were given to wear at a wedding can be a concrete symbol of that love, to be buried or laid under a tree. A symbol can be as simple as a rock that always reminds you of the lake where you spent your last vacation, or as complex as a crucifix.

Trees themselves embody an ancient archetype, their roots digging into the earth, their branches stretching toward the sun. The world tree, the center of creation, the joining of heaven and earth, is a universal symbol. Why not plant a tree as its representative here?

If you would feel a little silly stuffing archetypes into your garden, don't. Just play around with objects and meanings. Try a statue or a pottery bird hung from a branch, and if you don't like it, take it out and give it to a friend. Buy a toy airplane just because you like airplanes, and hang it from a tree. Perhaps it represents freedom from gravity. Perhaps it's just fun.

TRADITION

Gardens can also be places where important events happen. They provide sacred surroundings for baptisms, weddings, memorial services, and blessings of all kinds. The garden becomes a room where the earth, the wind, the sun, and the sea have their parts in your ceremony.

These occasions often bring us together with our families, which is always important. Ancestral traditions can be tied in with our gardens, from decorating a small tree for Christmas to using Halloween as the cutoff point for harvesting and weeding. Sharing a bit of whiskey with the trees on New Year's Day has possibilities, too.

Forget solemnity. Who sits around with friends pontificating? What touches our souls most deeply can be fun as well as meaningful, especially when kids are involved. Helping a three-year-old bury one Easter egg as a gift to the earth could never be dull. And you'll chuckle to yourself as you bury teeth the "tooth fairy" collected.

What other family traditions can be linked to a garden? Can you invent some new ones? Books of folklore often have ideas that can be resurrected. Just be sure they have an authentic meaning for you; rituals without meaning are simply busywork. Look for the ones that hit your heart, making you say, "Aha! That's it."

Questions to Guide You Deeper

What kind of garden space makes me feel the most at peace?

What would my ancestors have done to honor the earth?

What symbols of my religion are appropriate here?

What symbols turn up frequently in my dreams?

What colors have special meanings for me?

What parts of the earth do I want to invite into my garden?

Which animals are most important to me, and how can I bring them into the garden, symbolically?

We tend to think of our ancestors as offering rites out of fear, to appease the spirits of the land. We've forgotten the element of love that existed between people and the land they lived on for thousands of years, as close as the love between a child and its mother. We give gifts on Mother's Day. Why wouldn't they have offered gifts in the same spirit?

The Irish, for instance, sing love songs—praise songs—about particular bays and mountains. Other countries have similar traditions. Emigration cut off these ties, and those of us who are descendants of emigrants need to reestablish connections our ancestors took for granted.

And so we come round again to the question "What is the relationship we want to have with the earth?" and to the fact that our gardens embody this relationship, whatever it is. Intimate, personal, infuriating, frustrating, and always changing, our partnership with the earth touches us deeply.

PART THREE

Getting Your Hands in the Dirt

The art of lazy gardening is knowing when to act and when to watch, when to plant and when to have patience. Sometimes we avoid our gardens because we feel guilty for neglecting them, starting a downward spiral which usually results in chaos. Here are some ways to clear away the debris of guilt, an important first step in getting down to work, and, once you are outside, guidelines for both doing and not-doing.

Chapter Thirteen

Gardener's Guilt (and How to Cure It)

ou love plants, but there are eight new perennials sitting next to the garage that you bought and haven't had time to put in the ground. Half are almost dead, and the other half are so root-bound you'll have to cut them back before planting them. You don't want to look at them, or at the bed of lettuce you should have watered last week.

Your yard is a disaster and you're responsible. And you're caught in "Gardener's Guilt," a major obstacle to creating the garden you want, but curable if treated properly.

You could, for instance, pull or throw out everything that makes you feel guilty. You could bribe yourself into working. Or you could simply stand out in the middle of the yard, apologize for all your shortcomings, and ask for forgiveness. Crazy? Yes, but also effectively lazy.

Typical symptoms of Gardener's Guilt are paralysis, inability to make decisions, a desire to run away, a desire to sell the house and start over somewhere else, and an inability to look at any plant without feeling we should have done something for it and didn't.

Sound familiar? This disease is worse for your garden than any slug or fungus or weed. It attacks your pleasure, your delight in just being with plants. It needs to be eradicated whenever it takes root.

THE ANTIDOTES

First, whenever you think of something you "should" have done, tell yourself, "I don't have to do that if I don't want to." Who really cares if you didn't divide the daisies or pull the weeds out of the asparagus? The neighbors will survive if the lawn has a few dandelions, your visitors won't notice the new bed that would have been wonderful but isn't there, and the kids don't care if you didn't plant greens in the vegetable garden.

Do whatever you can to wipe your mental slate clean, absolutely spotless. You didn't have to do any of these things; you don't have to do any of them now. Then give yourself an hour to be in your yard, doing nothing, just looking at what's there. Sit down and watch the robins poking at worms, examine the primroses, or notice the shading on the rose leaves.

Often, we're simply to busy to stay in contact with our gardens. A week goes by, or two, and we've hardly gone outside except to walk to the car. I try to make a brief visit part of my waking-up routine, something to do while I'm drinking a cup of tea or coffee. It takes only a few minutes and gives me a rest from the pressure of a full morning schedule.

I'm convinced that most of the jobs we're supposed to do out here in the garden are simply excuses for spending time with the plants. After all, if your Puritan work ethic can't stand the thought of just sitting and watching the leaves sprout up in spring, you have to find things to do.

Such as weeding. There's plenty of time to look around while you're weeding and there are lots of opportunities to enjoy the earth, but why not skip the work on days when you're not in the mood and just enjoy? Think up a great reward for the weeding that *must* be done, put it on your calendar, and relax.

If you're caught up in Gardener's Guilt, you need to rebel. You have enough "shoulds" in your life, necessities that help you keep your job and your family together. Gardens aren't for "shoulds," they're for pleasure.

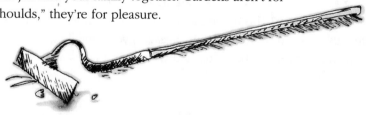

Or, as was discussed in the first chapter, gardens are for growing a partnership with the earth. How many of the chores you haven't done were necessary from the earth's point of view? How many were from your obsessively orderly great-aunt's?

Rethinking Neglect

Let's go back to basics. What looks like neglect on the surface—an inability to get yourself into proper gardening regimentation—can disguise a healthy desire for a different kind of garden, a garden where you play the part of admirer/lover rather than nurturer/controller.

Sometimes breaking down old ideas about gardening results in a period of chaos, when we're not quite sure what we want or what we need. We just know that weeding, watering, and fiddling around with endless trivialities doesn't work anymore.

Chores to Put Off Occasionally

Pulling out the weeds that sprout from seeds, not roots (see Chapter 18 for guidelines)

Cutting down old, withered stems

Fertilizing

Transplanting anything not in immediate danger

Dividing perennials

Ways to Enjoy Your Garden Instead

Try a taste of chickweed

Make a dried arrangement out of seedheads

Use a magnifying glass to look at the veins of a leaf

Lie on the grass with the sun warming your back

Pick flowers from different parts of the yard and plan new combinations

The problem is that you feel guilty because you don't fit the mold of "gardener." You feel there is something wrong with you; you just don't have a green thumb; you're lazy and disorganized.

Obviously, I'm speaking from experience. I don't think anyone has created as many disasters as I have, or felt more guilty. How could someone who loves plants, has spent years working with them, and gets so much enjoyment out of being around them have such a lousy garden?

Only after commiserating with a similarly neglectful friend did I realize the change of direction I needed to take. "Perhaps," she said, "we're wanting a garden where we respect nature. Perhaps we're really doing it right; it just doesn't look right yet."

This was the end of guilt and the beginning of gardening as experimentation. I have always had an itch to try what the books said not to do, just to see what happens. I've planted moisture-loving cowslips in dry shady grass and had them flourish. I've also lost more plants than I can count.

Mistakes Are Part of Learning

Who would scold a baby for falling down every time she started to walk? Why scold yourself for falling down occasionally?

Yes, neglecting the plants you've just bought is not the best way to garden. Allowing the quack grass to expand its territory for six months is not the best way to garden, either. You don't need to hear all that again.

What you need is respect for your gardening experiments. What did you learn from buying more plants than you wanted to use right this minute? Perhaps you needed to put them in different places around the yard, see how they fit, live with them a while before you made a final decision. Perhaps you needed to experiment with new colors that turned out not to fit with what you have. Perhaps you need to visit nurseries only when you have a day off.

Punishing yourself creates blocks against gardening. Looking at mistakes as part of the learning process opens you up to new possibilities, new ways of looking at the garden, and new ways of putting yourself into that frame. Give yourself the freedom to experiment, to explore, to try the unusual—the freedom to live without guilt.

What comes next? Building your garden, the way you built fascinating shapes out of blocks when you were a kid. Without the guilt, you can congratulate yourself on what you've created so far, then put on your old jeans and get ready to starting digging again.

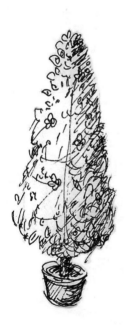

Chapter Fourteen

Getting Down to Work

N ow that you're out in the garden, where do you start? The number of tasks on your "to be done" list would take 20 hours to complete, but two are all you can spare from a busy schedule. When you walk out the door, the weeds to the right vie for your attention with the pruning to be done to your left. All you see is chaos.

Don't despair. There are ways to cut the work down to size, and, more importantly, ways to approach the garden with respect for your own rhythms and patterns.

You'll never be one of those people who start out on Saturday morning with a neat list of chores and finish it by noon. Why would you want to be? You have your own talents and gifts, unique characteristics that need their own kind of environment to flourish and bloom.

IMMEDIATE GRATIFICATION

Fun. Bright colors. Praise. Play. You need to allow yourself to be a preschooler again. If you feel silly, remember that creativity flows from this part of your personality. Celebrate it!

On the other hand, preschoolers need structure and a bit of discipline. Anarchy isn't really much fun. The trick is to balance playtime with clear boundaries.

Let's look at one of the most common complaints of lazy gardeners: "I did so much work but I don't feel like I've gotten anywhere." I've heard this from many, many people. They planted a tree here, a few vegetables over there, dug out the weeds in another place, and the yard still looks like a mess. There is no reward for their work.

Immediate gratification is a powerful incentive to do more. Use it. If you know your attention span is about 20 minutes, figure out how much beauty you can create in that time frame. If you buy the plants and soil beforehand, you can create a pot full of flowers. Or, if weeding is a must, don't just leave the soil bare: Use that space as an artist uses a canvas. Add some perennials, a few rocks, and some moss.

You need to admire your achievements as often as possible, so work on the most visible areas first. The front entry is important. Walk up to your door and imagine how it would look with a small bed of annuals next to it. Perhaps a clematis winding around the porch or a small tree sheltering the doorstep would feel welcoming.

Think about the view from your picture window. If you're traveling during the summer, perhaps a fall garden planted in gold, rust, and purple tones would be a better choice than July- or August-blooming perennials. A three-foot-square planting would take little time, but would act as a focal point for your view.

Once you have a few accomplishments to brag about, think of creative ways to inspire your inner child. If you were a teacher, how would you make garden jobs as easy and fun as possible?

Buying plants, for instance, is fun; dealing with them once you get them home is work. It's easy to simply put them down and say, "I'll plant them tomorrow." Tomorrow stretches into next week and, before you know it, they've become dry, root-bound, and scraggly.

A strict rule like "You must always plant the day you buy" won't work. You'll simply rebel, daring anyone to make you. What's needed is a bit of subtle planning. You know there won't be places for all of the plants; you know you'll need time to consider where each one will go. Why not have a holding bed in an out-of-the-way corner, some open ground ready for quick planting?

Everything can be planted close together, higgledy-piggledy, without thought or plan. Everything is easy to water, being in one spot. Everything is growing and is easy to transplant whenever you get the time.

You need a reward for getting your purchases into the ground the same day you bought them, if only an admiring "You really did a good job" addressed to yourself. We rarely praise ourselves, and yet we need the reassurance, the sense of being loved. Generous praise is one of the best balms we can give ourselves; apply it liberally.

For a more tangible reward, what about a candlelit dinner, or a long bubble bath? Make a list of pleasures to use as compensations for unaccustomed discipline. Even an uninterrupted half hour with a cup of coffee and a magazine can be a treat. Now, while you're working, think about how relaxed and virtuous you'll feel later.

STARTING SOMEWHERE

Another way to subtly guide yourself into the garden is to cultivate the fine art of puttering. Again, give yourself a firm half hour or so, free of phone calls and other distractions. Go outside and follow your intuition. Puttering asks for sensitivity to what calls you now, this minute.

You may start out by noticing the way dewdrops hang on a spider web or the light shines through a rhododendron blossom. Then you might want to pick the old brownish flowers off the side of the bush. After a few minutes, you see a clump of chickweed. It wouldn't hurt to remove it. Then you move on to something else.

Scattered? Yes, but you're there, in the garden, at liberty to do anything you want. Often you'll be tricked into a bit of needed pruning or tidying. The difference between puttering and work is the difference between freedom and responsibility. In puttering, any task is accomplished by accident rather than intention.

What Can Wait?

Now, let's look at that "to be done" list. Are there any chores there that could be crossed off entirely? Anything to do with future projects falls into this category. You'll be starting them later. Right now we're digging you out from under the past, giving you a fresh start.

Next, cross off anything that won't be the worse for a month's delay. If it won't shrivel, spread, grow too long to cut, or kill your trees, you can neglect it. In this case, follow the adage "Don't do tomorrow what you can put off until next week."

Now you're left with the emergencies. Imminent fatalities, usually for lack of watering, need to be handled first. Weeds whose seeds are almost ready to spill are next. The last thing you need are unwanted seedlings. Now what's left?

Help

Still in despair? One solution is to pay someone else to do what you can't. Why not? We think nothing of buying twice as many clothes as we need or shelves of books we could easily have borrowed from the library, but hiring someone to weed our garden? That's extravagant and an admission of our own failure to be self-sufficient, to handle it all.

But wouldn't a half-day's hard work by a professional erase most of that to-do list? I've been called often to come in as a sort of spring tonic, to get someone out from under jobs too hard or tedious to enjoy, to help them reestablish a sense of joy in their garden.

If you decide to call in some help, ask a good nursery for recommendations. Perhaps one of their part-time employees does pruning and weeding on the side, or they know a knowledgeable gardener who's looking for work. You might also try the horticulture department of a local community college. Sometimes they have students willing to work for less than more experienced professionals.

Don't wait until mid-spring to start calling around. Everyone is busy then. You'll have the best luck finding a skilled gardener in early spring or midsummer.

Be specific when giving directions to a gardener. Do you want every last weed pulled, or just the biggest ones? Do you want the whole yard weeded, or just two hours' worth? Do you need a general pruning of the whole garden, or just the fruit trees?

What if you prefer not to hire help? You could trade chores with a friend, or work on both gardens together, with plenty of gossip to lighten the burden. You could bribe your nephew to help in exchange for sailing lessons. Sit down and brainstorm your own list of possibilities.

Most important, cultivate enough patience to keep plugging at the list before you impulsively dig up the lawn for a new bed. Yes, it's just what you want most to create right now, but think lazy, lazy, lazy, patience, patience, patience.

Chapter Fifteen

How to Do It . . . If You Must

Do you feel like a fool when you walk through the garden center, listening to the salesperson talk about planting, fertilizing, and pruning? None of these is an esoteric discipline. With some understanding of plant processes, you can do what you must with confidence. *Must* is the key word. If it isn't essential—or fun—don't do it. You have plenty of other places to put your time. Here are some of the common skills and how to use them less.

PLANTING

Putting a small shrub or perennial in the ground and watching it expand into lush, vigorous maturity is a bit like watching a magic trick. Choosing the right plant helps, but it's essential to set it correctly. Don't skimp on work here; healthy plants need a proper start in life.

First read or reread the section in Chapter 2, pp. 13–16, on soil and roots. When a seed sprouts, the roots spread out into a wide network seeking water and nutrients for the plant. Newly planted roots need to establish the same broad, deep network as soon as possible. Roots are the foundation of all subsequent growth: Care for them as if they were priceless.

Dryness kills small roots quickly and root hairs almost immediately, so guard against it. Before you plant, make sure all the roots are moist. Water container plants ahead of time so they aren't soggy, and soak bare-root trees in water overnight.

Container plants won't lose any roots when moved into your garden; their leaves remain nourished and supported. Bare-root and balled and burlapped trees and shrubs probably left a few behind, so the immediate need is to establish a balance between the roots and the foliage. Otherwise, the leaves may wilt or become stunted.

You don't need to cut back the main structure of the plant; you do need to take off a quarter to half of the leaf area for best growth. This means picking off lower leaves and pruning off small, unimportant branches. If you want a fruit tree to stay low and wide, top the tallest branches, cutting them back to a side shoot. Now you're ready to plant.

The ground should be moist, but not wet. Wet soil packs together, destroying the pattern of spaces that allow air and water to reach the roots. Wait until the ground dries out a bit, then get your shovel or trowel and begin.

Dig a hole about twice the size of the root ball, then loosen the soil at the sides and bottom. Bare-root trees and shrubs need no extra soil preparation if you've chosen your varieties well. Container and balled and burlapped specimens can be given a little improvement with manure and other organic matter, if you choose, as a way of helping them make the transition from one soil to another.

Take the plant out of the pot or bag it came in, and set it in the hole so that the top of the root ball is even with the surface of the surrounding soil. If you plant too deep, the roots may be smothered; rhododendrons and azaleas are particularly sensitive. If you plant too high, the root ball will dry on top, killing those roots and wicking water away from the lower ones, too.

Spread out the roots as much as possible. Tight, wound roots will stay like that, and a tight, small root system will be unable to support good growth. Fill the spaces between roots with soil, pushing it in with your fingers to get rid of any air pockets. If you have light, sandy or highly organic soil, push firmly. If you have heavier clay soil, pat it in lightly, then water to help it settle.

Water your new acquisition with a solution including rooting hormone and a small amount of liquid fertilizer. This settles the soil and gives the roots a beginning boost; it will also foster strong root systems, your best defense against disease.

Fertilize again in a few weeks with a 5-10-10 compound (5 percent nitrogen, 10 percent phosphorus, and 10 percent potassium) and give the newly freed root system enough water without drowning it. Then gradually withdraw your artificial support and let it take off on its own. (See page 103 for more detailed information on fertilizers.)

Roots will grow slowly during winter if the ground isn't frozen, giving a fall-planted tree or shrub a larger root system to meet the stresses of summer heat. Plant in the early fall to take advantage of this growth. One problem: In the fall, nurseries rarely have the selection of plants they stock in spring. If you're landscaping a difficult-to-water area such as a hillside, one where spring plantings may not survive, and the species you want aren't available in fall, you may need to buy in spring and plant in an easy-to-water holding bed. By the rainy season they'll have large, healthy root systems. Place them in their permanent positions at that time and they should withstand some drought the following summer. How can you spend less time planting? Spend more time planning. Do whatever it takes to get exactly the right plant for each spot. Yes, there are always mistakes, but that's part of life. Just look before you leap into a spring planting frenzy.

TRANSPLANTING

When you dig up a tree or shrub and move it to another spot in your garden, some of the roots are left behind. Be sure to remove at least half the leaves to balance this loss; you'll have new ones before you know it. Again, you don't have to cut back the main branches. Just take off little ones and pick off most of the lower leaves. Nothing stops a plant from settling into its new home like having its root structure—the plant's support system—reduced by half, while its top growth remains the same.

To decrease root loss, take as large a root ball as possible. If you can plan ahead, dig down around the shrub a few weeks beforehand; new roots will form within the cut. When you have to move something large, with a wide-ranging root system—larger than a few feet in diameter—cut half the roots in a semicircle six months ahead of time and the other side three months later. This process, called root pruning, ensures that you'll have a compact, successful root ball when it's time to move.

Some root systems are small, barely extending beyond the leaves, while some extend far beyond the drip line, the imaginary circle on the ground directly under the tips of the outermost branches. Some are close to the surface; others go down six feet or more. If you're not sure which kind you're dealing with, it pays to do a little exploratory digging long before you have to root prune.

Timing is critical to moving plants. Do it during a hot spell and you may have a wilted, half-dead tree in a week, even after leaf removal. Do it in early spring or late fall, and the same tree will probably settle in fine.

In an emergency, however, you can break the rules. If a bulldozer is going to obliterate an heirloom rose anyway, why not try an August move? Take off almost all the leaves and dig a huge root ball, bigger than you can carry, if necessary. Hose off some of the dirt, partially bare-rooting it, if the ball is too heavy. Keep all the exposed roots wet until you have the root ball safely in the ground again, then water well for several weeks using rooting hormone solution.

WATERING

Learn to water wisely. This means soaking the soil to the depth of the lowest roots, encouraging them to go deeper and wider, then letting the ground dry out for a while, discouraging the growth of surface roots. You'd be surprised at how deep roots can grow, up to six feet in tomatoes and one-and-one-half to two feet in lawn grasses.

Water most diligently when new growth is expanding; the need for water is greatest then. Allow the soil around trees and shrubs to dry in late summer and fall, encouraging a natural hardening-off process before winter.

Water in the morning so leaves will have a chance to dry off before evening, reducing the risk of fungus diseases that might get started on warm, moist leaves.

Finally, be prepared to give extra attention to newly planted trees and shrubs. Even those from the driest climates can't handle immediate neglect; their root systems are too small. If your climate is mild, plant in fall so that the roots take hold before spring. Otherwise, plant as early as possible and water diligently the first summer, occasionally the next.

How can you cut down on the need to keep track of the weather and the moisture in the soil? Control your urge to plant whatever strikes your fancy. If you fix firm standards for drought resistance, you'll free yourself from this chore.

Watering Container Plants

Watering is a continual chore with containers. Water-holding granules, plastics that expand when wet, can be added to your soil mix to give yourself some extra time between soakings. You can also set up a drip system if you're well organized. Otherwise, be motherly and solicitous with your pots; there's nothing more depressing than dead plants. A plant in a clay or terra cotta container looks more elegant, but dries out much faster than one in a plastic pot.

How do you know when to water? Stick your finger down into the soil; if it feels dry an inch down you can flood it. Excess water will flow down and out the drainage holes at the bottom of your pot. Never plant in a kettle or other solid-bottomed container; the water has no place to exit, air can't get into the soil spaces, the roots suffocate and then rot. For the same reason, place the pot on small stones if you're using a saucer beneath it. Otherwise, water will pool in the bottom inch of soil, again causing root rot.

FERTILIZING

What is a fertilizer? It's something added to the soil to give the roots extra nutrients to transmit to the rest of the plant. Some fertilizers are inorganic chemical compounds, usually fast-acting, and others are plant and animal materials that are naturally high in various useful chemicals. Some are ground-up rocks that break down slowly into forms of nutrient available to the roots.

The three seemingly secret numbers on every box or bag of fertilizer stand for the percentages of nitrogen, phosphorus, and potassium in the mix. These are the most widely used substances to stimulate growth. Added nitrogen produces lush green leaves, but few flowers or fruit. These are induced by the second two elements. In other words, if you want to get lots of leaves and branches, add nitrogen. If you want lots of flowers and fruit, add a fertilizer higher in phosphorus and potassium.

There are a variety of reasons to fertilize and a corresponding variety of materials to suit them. So, the first step is to be clear about why you're doing this.

Are you transplanting a shrub? Use a balanced fertilizer to get both roots and leaves growing. Are you starting lettuce and spinach? Pick one with lots of nitrogen for leaf growth. Are you planting tulips and crocuses? They need phosphorus and potassium to regenerate bulbs each year; choose long-lasting bone meal.

Liquid fertilizers give quick growth, but be careful not to over-stimulate. A beautifully lush shrub may not have the hardiness it needs to survive the winter, while a slow but steadily growing specimen may do just fine. Also, adding too much fertilizer causes leaf burn, a browning or blackening of the leaves.

Are you fertilizing to get a ground cover to fill in solidly? Go for fast coverage with liquid fertilizers in spring and early summer, then forget the feeding so they'll harden off.

Are you making a permanent change in some dreary, impoverished soil? Get the slowest-acting fertilizers you can find, and use a lot. You'll never burn the roots with ground-up rock or bones.

Do you want to improve your soil's ability to retain water and nutrients? Add organic matter such as manure, ground leaves, or homemade compost. Compost is wonderful but lazy gardeners can rarely get their kitchen scraps onto a pile, much less turn it weekly. If you have some extra energy, try this method. Keep a pile of sawdust handy in a garbage pail, layer it with soft, watery material (like old lettuce or leftover soup greens) and lawn clippings, then sit back and wait. Decay will be slow but eventually you'll have rotted, crumbly compost to add to your garden.

Are you planting pots of annuals to brighten your deck? A pelleted, slow-release fertilizer is a wise addition. Confined roots do need extra feeding, and this is the easiest way to give it. While it's not cheap, your mind is freed from a weekly or biweekly fertilizing schedule.

How can you use less fertilizer? Plant only what matches your soil. If it's poor soil, search out the trees, shrubs, and perennials that do just fine in that kind of environment. Use fertilizers only when necessary and for specific purposes. If a plant is doing well, leave it alone.

Organic Fertilizers

Commercially blended fertilizers come in combinations formulated for specific purposes. Here is a list of organic fertilizers with their NPK (Nitrogen-Phosphorus-Potassium) ratios so you can customize your own mixture.

Blood meal 13-1-0: quick acting, promotes leafy growth

Feather meal 12-1-0: slow-acting, promotes leafy growth

Bone meal 3-15-0: for bulbs and blossoms, provides calcium also

Cottonseed meal 6-2-1: for leafy growth of acid-loving plants

Kelp meal 0-0-2: also has trace nutrients, valuable for most plants

Fish meal 10-4-0: readily available nutrients, promotes leafy growth

Alfalfa meal 3-2-2: especially good for roses

Sunflower hull ash 0-0-34: often used for growing potatoes in potassium-deficient soils

Rock phosphate 0-27-0: also contains 24% calcium and 29% magnesium

PRUNING

Why are you picking up those pruning shears? "Why" is the essential word, and the answer determines when and how you'll use them.

The most common reason is that a shrub has gotten too big and is blocking the picture window or the front walkway. This is either because of poor planning (a six-foot-wide bush stuffed into a three-foot-wide space) or because the shrub is fifteen years old and still growing. In the first case, you can certainly reduce the shrub's size, but you'll be forced to repeat the process yearly. Consider replacing it with something smaller. In the second, an occasional removal of the branches extending farthest will keep it within bounds.

In either instance, prune large branches back to the center, allowing smaller ones to take over. Many people cut six inches off the top and sides, leaving a hacked-off wreck that never recovers its graceful form. Don't.

Wise pruning involves an understanding of how branches grow. Typically, each main branch sprouts a varying number of side branches; it ends in a bud at its tip. If you cut the main branch back to one of the side branches, it will take over the function of the main branch. If a cut is made to the center of any branch, to a bare area or one with a few leaves, four or five branch shoots will develop below it from dormant buds that begin to grow.

This is fine if you want branches—if you wish to create a shrub that's full and bushy—but disastrous in a tree, for instance, that should keep a graceful, willowy form. Know what your goal is and prune accordingly.

It's essential to make a clean, sharp cut. The thin green tissue just underneath the bark, the cambium, is the actively growing layer that will heal the wound. If the edge of the cut is ragged, healing takes more time and the wound is more vulnerable to disease.

Always cut just above a bud—not too close, or the bud may be damaged, but close enough to allow the small stub to heal. Growth energy will be diverted into the bud; any stretch of stem beyond it will die. Sometimes this death will include tissue below your new branch, weakening it.

Fruit trees have certain specific requirements. I recommend that you consult a book devoted to that subject if you intend to plant one, then decide if yearly pruning is a chore for which you have time.

Ground covers can benefit from a pruning in their early stages, a shearing back that is designed to produce more shoots and better coverage of the soil. I prefer to do this branch by branch—a slow process, perhaps, but one that results in a more attractive planting. You can also take hedge shears to the plants and wait for the new growth to hide the stubs.

Many trees look more elegant if some of the lower branches are removed as they grow older, exposing the trunk and main branches to give them a more treelike silhouette. Large shrubs can often be pruned into small trees using this method. The growth energy will be channeled into the canopy, giving more height, also.

When should you prune? If you're taking branches off a flowering shrub, timing is important. Early spring flowers, such as forsythia, come from buds created last year; prune these plants right after blooming.

Summer flowers, such as roses, come from buds set on new shoots; prune these just before growth starts.

Other pruning can be more sporadic. Early spring is traditional, but late summer does quite well. Wounds heal fast then, and there is less likelihood of sucker growth getting out of hand if you prune back severely. Suckers are long, narrow shoots going straight up that spoil a tree's shape and take energy away from the main framework. They usually sprout after severe topping, but can appear any time. Cut them off whenever you see them.

Pruning conifers can be tricky; cut back too far and all you have is a bare stub. If you must control growth (and please consider planting something else instead), taking small bites out of the new growth is best. The long "candles" of pines, the new growth, can be cut in half or removed entirely. Firs and hemlocks can be cut back to side branches. Still, this is a yearly chore best avoided.

How can you do less pruning? Plant appropriate sizes and shapes for your space. Impatience may suggest that you get a fast-growing species that fills a blank spot quickly, but that's only asking for trouble later. Again, patience is best.

PROPAGATING

If you're going to fuss around with propagation—growing new plants from seeds or cuttings—be sure to consider whether the money you save is worth the time you spend. Some methods are easy and nearly carefree. Others are fun but best left to others if you want to save time.

Sowing

The easiest, most rewarding method is sowing seeds directly into the ground in fall or early spring, when rains take care of the watering. This technique works only with plants that don't mind frost. There are plenty of these; see Chapter 8 for some suggestions.

You don't want weeds competing with your seedlings. Clear the planting area a few weeks ahead of time. Any weeds that sprout can be hoed off when they are small, leaving clear ground for the flowers you want.

Fine seeds can be mixed with sand to keep them from clumping, then broadcasted (scattered) over the top of the soil. Press them in with your hand or a board, and then water. Larger seeds need to be covered with a quarter inch or so of soil, but can still be broadcast rather than pushed in individually.

Sowing seeds indoors and planting them outside, or sowing tender annuals outside when you're in charge of the watering, can be rewarding or depressing, depending on your diligence with the hose. When the weather is hot, seedlings dry out more quickly than you'd expect; hourly sprinklings are often needed (don't let the surface of the ground dry out). On the plus side, you can grow hundreds of plants from a packet of seeds costing a dollar or two. It's your decision.

Dividing

Dividing is one technique that is often quick and easy enough to justify the trouble. Usually used with perennials or bulbs whose crowns (clusters of buds) get larger each year, dividing consists of separating these growing points and their associated roots, then replanting. Be sure to take off half of the leaves to balance the loss of roots.

Some plants, such as Shasta daisies, can be pulled apart with your fingers; others may need a knife. Dense masses of stems and roots, such as those of the Siberian iris, can be cut into two or three pieces using a sharp shovel. The key point to remember is that each cluster of roots should have a bud or tuft of leaves at the top. Plant each section (firming soil around the roots), mulch with about an inch of bark or other material, then soak. If done in early spring when rains can water the new plants, you should have quick new growth to reward you.

Cuttings

Taking cuttings, small pieces of stem that root and become independent, can also be easy and quick. The success rate varies from species to species, from willow wands that can simply be stuck in the ground to rhododendron cuttings that require special greenhouse conditions. Some may root in water; others need to be dipped in rooting hormone and inserted to about half their length in sand. I've had the best luck with the latter method. A plastic bag can be placed over the cuttings to keep the humidity high, and when roots show you can plant them into soil.

Plants That Root Easily from Cuttings

Geranium (*Pelargonium*), *Impatiens, Dianthus,* red-stem dogwood (*Cornus stolonifera*), willow (*Salix*), penstemon, kinnikinick (*Arctostaphylos uva-ursi*), juniper (*Juniperus*), English laurel (*Prunus laurocerasus*), yew (*Taxus*), and *Spiraea.*

When clipping a stem for cuttings, try to include three or four buds, usually found at the base of leaves. Slice the bottom just below one of these and remove all but the top cluster of leaves. If these are large, ship off half of each to reduce wilting.

With some shrubs and trees, timing of cuttings is critical. New, soft growth won't root, so cuttings are usually taken from August into winter. Consult a plant encyclopedia for information about specific species.

Layering

There are a number of other propagation methods, but the easiest is layering. Used on shrubs whose lower branches nearly touch the ground, it simply involves making a cut on the lower surface of the branch where it is nearest the ground. Place a matchstick or other small piece of wood in the cut to keep it open, weight the branch, and cover the area with soil. Then wait. In six months to a year, enough roots will have formed from the cut that you can remove the branch and plant it on its own, as a new shrub. The same method can be used on higher branches, but the cut must be surrounded by moist peat or sphagnum moss and a layer of plastic.

How can you do less propagating? Spend the money to buy new plants someone else has grown. The balance depends on your own budget and time.

Chapter Sixteen

Starting a Garden from Scratch

A blank canvas is a gift, with opportunities for unhindered creativity. However, a new house set in an expanse of dirt looks just that: blank. The impulse to immediately plant something—anything—may be irresistible. Don't give in to it.

Many times during my years of odd-job gardening I've been called in to remedy disasters, and most of them started right here. Quick, impulsive, scattered plantings beg for improvement. Huge beds installed all at once without maintenance become weedy monstrosities. Getting back to the blank canvas becomes nearly impossible.

INVEST IN YOUR SOIL

What is your biggest problem and your greatest opportunity? Soil. Left bare, nature will try to cover it with whatever is handy, generally dandelions and thistles. Tractors and bulldozers have probably left it hardened and compressed. You're lucky if any topsoil remains.

On the other hand, never again will you have the same chance to loosen the soil deeply, add organic matter, and create the healthiest soil possible. I always try to match plants with the soil they prefer rather than change soil to suit a finicky plant, but this opportunity is too good to miss.

I once met a man in his sixties who had just spent two years improving the soil in his yard, without planting a thing. At 28, I couldn't conceive of that kind of patience. As I get older, however, I find myself longing for that chance.

Why? Because good soil, deep and receptive to roots, is the foundation for healthy plants. It doesn't have to be rich in nutrients. Many shrubs and trees can survive well with a lean diet. Well-loosened soil, though, with enough organic matter to hold water, is a gift.

If you haven't been given that gift for free, however, consider investing work into it. A quick-fix solution is to cover the entire yard with a thick layer of organic matter, such as ground bark or sawdust, four to five inches, then turn it under. Add 50 pounds of 10-10-10 fertilizer with slow-release nitrogen and micronutrients for each three cubic yards of material. Hire whatever machinery will dig this in the deepest and give the soil a thorough mixing. Plant immediately.

While you're going to so much trouble, add some bone meal and lime if your climate produces acid soil. This is your only chance to work the soil widely and deeply; make the most of it.

Whatever you do, don't just get a few loads of topsoil and dump it over the hardened ground. If you were a root, would you go down into that stuff? No, you'd stay in the few inches of pleasant surroundings on top, vulnerable to a week's dry weather, never getting a good foundation.

The best long-term plan, however, is to plant green manures, quick-growing crops that are turned under when one to two feet tall, adding organic matter and breaking up the soil at the same time. Leave them to rot for a few weeks before planting anything else. Winter rye is one of the best, as its prodigious root growth thoroughly loosens compacted soil.

There are advantages to this method: You're letting nature's rock-breaking tools, roots, do your work for you; and the depth these roots can reach (two to three feet) is far deeper than any Rototiller™ or plow.

Green Manures

To sow in summer: buckwheat, oats, nondormant alfalfa (*Medicago sativa*), soybean, mustard

To sow in fall: Austrian field peas, common vetch, hairy vetch, crimson clover, winter rye, winter wheat, Tyfon (edible turnip–rape cross), fava beans

The main disadvantage is that you'll have to wait three months to a year to start working on your yard, depending on how many sowings you do.

Or *is* it a disadvantage? Your soil is happy under a blanket of growth, unlikely to sprout dandelions and dock. There is nothing pushing for your immediate attention. Now you have the leisure to plan.

LEISURELY PLANNING

Chapter 2 details the observations of sun, rain, wind, and soil patterns you need to make and recommends taking a year to do them. Compiling a list of possible plants for your site can occupy the same amount of time, if done thoroughly. That year you now have. Relax and enjoy it.

What a luxury, to plan, research, design, and play around with ideas without maintaining a garden at the same time! Perhaps only those who have had to live with hasty mistakes can appreciate this indulgence. Rectifying disasters can be exhausting; planning can be fun.

On the other hand, your hands itch to get into the ground, rows of blooming petunias and marigolds for sale are nearly irresistible, and you want to do something. What's the cure for spring fever?

Plant Pots

Plant pots full of herbs, of trailing lobelia and geraniums, or of strawberries. Plant pots of ferns and hostas together for shady corners. Plant a miniature rose in a graceful Italian pot by the front door.

This is where garden center annuals really come into their glory. You can stuff a number of them into a container, watch them bloom prodigiously all summer, and then you're done with them. There's no lingering guilt; they're gone.

If you're planting more than a few pots, buy your potting soil in large quantities. As discussed in Chapter 2, you can greatly improve potting soil by mixing it in a garbage can or wheelbarrow with some garden soil, some steer manure, and some other organic matter such as fine bark. The packaged soil mix will have peat moss, which is hard to moisten when dry, so I always add a few other organics to balance it out.

Get the largest containers you can afford; small ones dry out quickly. Inexpensive fiber pots are available for short-term use, or you can invest in lovely terra cotta ones. Remember, though, that clay dries out more quickly than plastic.

Whiskey barrels are big enough to hold small trees, but the metal bands around them eventually rust and break. I like the plain black pots nurseries use for shrubs and trees; you can get them occasionally just for the asking, or the nursery may be able to order some for you.

While the Grass Grows. . .

So now you have a container garden enhancing your new home, and the soil is broken up and improved to your satisfaction. What's next?

Get back to covering up the soil, this time with lawn or mulch. Grass will keep out most of the weeds, so seed it everywhere except in areas that you can plant immediately. It's easy to remove when you need to carve out new beds, so don't worry about covering up areas where shrubs or trees are planned. Your main concern now is minimizing bare soil.

By now you should have a solid plan sketched out, an image in your mind of what this yard will look like in five years. Your next task is step-by-step transfer of this image to the actual site. What are your first priorities?

Hard-to-mow slopes need mulch to keep the soil from crusting and shedding water, creating mini-streams that erode the soil. As soon as possible, plant a ground cover with a dense, strong root system for permanent stability; Chapter 7 lists several possibilities. Since slopes are so difficult to water, plant in fall or very early spring.

Trees need to be planted early to gain growth and size. You don't need to install a whole bed around it right now; just clear a patch equal to twice the width of the root ball. Loosen the soil, plant, and mulch.

Next, focus on the high-visibility areas, the ones next to the front and back doors or along the driveway. Take them in manageable chunks, a weekend project at a time. This is play time, like building with blocks. You should be able to try a piece here, a piece there, change your mind, and have fun.

Try to gather your materials before you start; nothing is more frustrating that not having the right toys. Buy the plants, mulch, rocks, fountain, or whatever and have them sitting right there, ready to be artistically arranged. You're not an artist? Any kid can have fun making a dish garden; you're no different.

First, install the "skeleton," the lines and objects you chose in Chapter 5. Use a hose to set out the line of the bed; add rocks or driftwood, or the fountain you've always wanted. Walk around, look at them from different angles, and make changes. Congratulate yourself on doing a great job.

Now place the plants, still in their containers, around the bed. Keep moving them around until the whole arrangement feels right, then dig holes for each and set them in. Pour yourself a glass of wine, and stand back and admire. Show off your creation to a friend. Boast about it.

Then decide which section you'll tackle next, either tomorrow or next year. The timing is your choice. You should be feeling so good about what you've accomplished that you have lots of energy for moving on to the next project. This energy is priceless; it's what you lose when you plant piecemeal, here and there, never feeling a sense of completion. Cultivate it as you would a fine rose.

Chapter Seventeen

Redoing an Existing Garden

What do you do with the monster you've already created, or inherited along with your house? Perhaps there are beds you half planted that happily continued to fill themselves with sheep's sorrel, dandelions, and dock. Perhaps the yard was planted 20 years ago and the foundation planting is over your head.

You may not know what many of the plants are, much less what to do with them. Taming this garden will take work at first, Saturday afternoons and long summer evenings of pruning and cleanup. However, your perseverance will pay off as you uncover the bones of an older garden.

Before you start stripping away excess flesh in the form of weeds and unwanted shrubs, take a few moments to consider the advantages of starting over again. Gardens from scratch, from bare ground, take years to achieve a settled look. They're gawky, frustrating places of potential for three or four years.

On the other hand, you have some maturity to work with. There are probably a few plants tall enough to be called trees. There are probably perennials that could be divided into enough individuals to fill a small bed. There is likely a scattering of flowering shrubs whose company you enjoy.

TAKING STOCK

The first step in rejuvenating this garden is to take inventory, to mark where the crocuses come up, to identify the odd-shaped leaves appearing out of nowhere in April and the shrubs that bloom in summer. If you've just bought the property, the process may take a year. It's time well spent.

Plants are expensive, and mature trees and shrubs are priceless. An expanse of daffodils worth hundreds of dollars can be ruined by careless digging when the bulbs are dormant. And who wants to be told by a neighbor that the dull bush you just destroyed was blooming with gold flowers last winter?

Photographs can be quick records of each month's changes, serving the purpose of a journal without requiring as much organization. They also aid the planning stage, cataloging colors and heights as well as time of bloom.

While you're observing your garden, note which specimens you want to keep and which you'd rather discard. Nagging dislikes for certain plants don't diminish; take out the orange azalea and the scrubby apple if they irritate you. You're not stuck with old mistakes, yours or someone else's.

There is a third category, however. This one is for plants you want to take out eventually, but that have use as place holders right now. They aren't your favorites, but you can live with them for a few years. As the new trees you plant gain size and breadth, you can take the old ones out without giving your garden a barren look.

MAKING THE MOST OF WHAT YOU HAVE

Go back to chapters 4 and 5. Create your design; choose the boundaries you'll work within. This is hard work, perhaps the toughest gardening you'll ever have to do, especially when you have a yard whose character is already formed. You could change that character, but how much time and energy is it worth?

Taking the garden you have now, removing what you must and working with what you have left, is an art. Perhaps the best approach is to focus on creating the most beautiful garden possible with what you've been given. Not that you shouldn't put your own dreams into reality, but an acceptance of the constraints, of what simply exists, gives you the freedom to transform those constraints into beauty.

Perhaps you'd rather not have the maple that dwarfs your house, but removing it wouldn't be right either. Accepting the fact that the house will look like a small cottage no matter what you do gives you the possibility of creating an extraordinary cottage, an extension of the cottage archetype toward perfection.

Many factors are simply givens, part of the frame within which we work. These include your style of house, the fact of city or country surroundings, the size and shape of your lot, and even the trees on your neighbor's land—the ones that become part of your "borrowed scenery."

Truly beautiful gardens have a sense of appropriateness, a harmony with their surroundings. Limiting? Perhaps, but there are plenty of places to be creative within those limits. Focus your playfulness on filling in the details; your broad outlines need to fit within the framework you're given.

Order from Chaos

After the hard work of planning, you need some immediate rewards. One of the quickest is edging all the beds. Neat edges make even the most chaotic planting scheme seem under control, intentional. My favorite way to do this is to remove a strip of sod several inches wide, leaving a six-inch-deep trench between the grass and the bed. Even quack grass finds it hard to jump across that gap.

Pruning is often dramatically transforming. Opening up the center of a tree reveals a well-proportioned pattern of branches. Taking out the tallest shoots of a forsythia at the base reveals an arching silhouette. Even removing gangly rhododendron branches renews the bush.

Cut down or pull out everything on your "To Remove" list. Hire someone if you need to. Get out from under the dead weight of unwanted growth. You'll feel lighter, free.

Weeds come next. For now, haul them out as quickly as you can. You need to see results. Later, you can go back and get the roots of the villains who sprout from each piece left behind. For the present, just make yourself feel good about the garden.

There's an art to balancing immediate results with long-term gains. Go too far into present gratification and you'll never have the loveliness you've planned. Go too far into practical plodding and you'll bore yourself right out of the garden. Go in one direction, then the other. Mix work with fun, planting marigolds with weeding.

LONG-TERM PLANNING

Once you've made the yard look as presentable as possible, it's time to work on the long-term plan. You haven't got one? Go back to chapters 4 and 5. Take all the time you need to think this through; you want every shovelful of dirt you haul to count. As you learned from the disaster you just cleaned up, recovery from mistakes is costly.

Now, in what sequence do you install your plan? Key plants that need to grow into their role come first; put in the maple that will shade your kitchen and the wisteria that will cover your deck. Then get your "skeleton" set, adding rocks, paths, arbor, and pond. Now move into planting your high-visibility areas, the entry and front beds. Create the focal points visible from the kitchen window and the back door. Then you can relax and do whatever you please next.

Transform one tiny piece, then another, then the next. Soon you'll have roses arching over the fence and pot marigolds instead of weeds along your paths. Slowly, gradually, changes will spread over the entire yard.

How do you find time for all this? Make setting up a bed a family project, or a way to chat with a friend. Work up your own creative solutions, but don't ever expect to have all the time you want. Use your free moments to guard your newly transformed areas against quack grass and dandelions. You may never have enough time to go back and do it all again.

Chapter Eighteen

Weeds

High on most people's list of unpleasant jobs is weeding. Many of us have a secret feeling that our garden is somehow being unfair, that it should only produce plants we like, none we don't. And that, of course, is the definition of a weed: a plant we don't want.

This weed might be a lovely thing in itself, even welcomed into other people's gardens, but when it starts taking over our garden we pull it out.

A MATTER OF PERSPECTIVE

I've heard ladies at garden club meetings exclaim, "Oh, but that's a weed!" when I've talked about an annual or perennial that is particularly generous with its seedlings. Forget-me-nots, violets, harebells, foxgloves, and Welsh poppies are all guilty of this kind of behavior. I, for one, appreciate it.

Perhaps it's an issue of control. Vagrant flowers disturb our sense of neatness and orderliness, our dream of creating exactly what we desire.

Or perhaps we have expectations of leaving nature alone and having it produce something like an archetypal mountain meadow. We love flowers; we deserve beauty.

The reality is that we have preferences and desires. Nature has forces and ecological principles. The trick is to meet nature's need for a green covering with plants that *you* choose. Or with leaves, pine needles, or something else. Satisfy the earth's basic need and you can be in control again, satisfying your own desire for beauty.

Mulches are fine for awhile, but something is going to grow there eventually. Organic materials decay, becoming fertile ground. Stones or pebbles always seem to host weeds eventually, and weeding them out is a nightmare. You'd be better off planting a ground cover, surrounding it by whatever mulch is cheapest in your area, and letting it fill in to make a solid mat.

But we'll leave redoing the garden for another time, another chapter. What about the disaster that's staring you in the face right now?

Weeding Can Be Fun?

Try combining weeding with something you enjoy. You might trade weeding parties with a friend who is similarly burdened; stimulating conversation is one of my favorite additions.

Music is another option. Take the boom-box outside and put on one of your favorite albums. Or try a cup of tea, adding some cookies for an occasional break.

Offer yourself a reward for good behavior. A morning's hard work really does deserve lunch at your favorite restaurant. Or, if you have a serious case of weeding phobia, plan something special after just an hour's work—perhaps a glass of wine or beer, or 10 minutes of blowing bubbles across the lawn. Try something silly, something fun.

So now you're out in the garden, trying to decide where to start. The first priority is your most visible area, the place you pass by almost every day. This might be the bed next to the front door or the one in front of the picture window, the one with the stunted, yellow shrubs you've been ignoring.

This step is important. At the end of a few hours, you'll have a clear, orderly patch of ground. You should be able to congratulate yourself frequently on your accomplishment, allowing it to give you confidence and energy to move on to the next problem. Remember, your own satisfaction is the best harvest.

Stick to one small section at a time. An hour's work concentrated in one place brings order into chaos; scattered bits of cleared ground bring frustration.

WEEDING TECHNIQUES

Weeding has its fine points, though everyone assumes the craft is common knowledge. Techniques include grab-everything-you-see-and-pull, cut-the-roots-with-a-knife, and dig-it-out-with-a-shovel. The major difference is in how much of the root growth is left in the soil. How diligent you need to be in removing roots depends on the type of weed.

If you're not familiar with the common weeds in your area, consult your neighbors, perhaps the retired couple down the street who tend their yard so devotedly. Pay for advice if you have to, but don't tear the garden apart without a guide.

Most annoying, and most important to remove, are the weeds that sprout up from any bit of root left in the ground. These include quack grass, comfrey, sheep sorrel, horsetail, and morning glory.

Quack grass, known in Britain as couch grass, has long white runners that always seem to leave pieces behind whenever they're pulled up. Each piece grows another plant, and a month later you're back where you started. Their runners have the power to break through weed cloth and plastic, infiltrate dense root systems, and even grow through small bulbs. (To be fair, however, I should point out that the seventeenth-century herbalist Culpeper so respected the root's medicinal value that he once said, "although a gardener be of another opinion, yet a physician holds half an acre of them to be worth five acres of carrots twice told over.")

Other than sifting all the soil in the bed, the best technique is to dig out all of the runners you can, then a week later pull up the new starts before they have a chance to root well. I even advise taking every plant out of a bed infested with quack grass and moving them to another spot for holding until they can be replanted. Dig over the bed two or three times, until nothing sprouts for two weeks, and then replant.

This doesn't sound very lazy, does it? Well, with plants that spread by runners, you have few choices. You can get all of them out, you can abandon the bed, or you can sell the place. Or you can simply pull them up, over and over again, for years, taking only the tops and some of the roots, never getting rid of them. Take your choice.

Deep-rooted plants, such as dandelion, thistle, and dock, are the next priority. Everyone knows what dandelions look like; thistles

announce their presence with prickles. Dock has
up to a foot of long oval leaves, with reddish mid-
ribs. All have taproots that may go down to
one-and-a-half feet in older plants. They're
tough to dig out completely, and the buried

tip you missed will sprout up again. Since they don't spread wildly, you
can be more tolerant, but getting them young saves work.

Deep-rooted weeds respond best to having the ground around
them loosened with a digging fork; the root can then slide out easily.
Small ones can be handled with a trowel, but you run the risk of leaving
half the root behind when your tool is too short.

Other weeds can be regarded with a certain amount of tolerance.
Try to get them out before they flower, since the last thing you want is
more seeds, but then, who's going to get upset about a bit of chickweed
or shepherd's purse among the daisies?

HERBAL AND EDIBLE WEEDS

Of course, one of the laziest ways to deal with weeds in your garden is to
change your attitude and start eating them. Almost all the common of-
fenders are edible—as greens, usually—or can be used medicinally.

Herbalists find virtue in many despised plants. Self-heal, plantain,
Klamath weed (also known as Saint Johnswort), chickweed, dock, and
nettles are all used for healing. Invite an herbalist to visit your yard if
you want to appreciate your weeds instead of pull them.

Dandelion greens are a commonly recommended addition to salads. I've found that those growing in shade develop larger, less bitter
leaves than those in full sun. Seeds of particularly good strains are available also.

You could run your own breeding program for other weeds, se-
lecting the largest, best-tasting ones and letting them reseed. But before
you start cooking with plants that appear in your garden, get a field
guide to edible wild plants. You don't want to get a poisonous foxglove
leaf mixed up in your salads.

Many weeds are annuals, covering ground quickly by spreading
lots of seed. You can mimic their behavior with more ornamental plants

Weeding Tools

Kitchen knife: Buy one at a thrift store, with a blade six to eight inches long. This is useful for most weeds when getting all the roots out isn't essential.

Trowel: Useful for small weeds and sandy soil.

Weeder: A long shaft with a sharpened end, this can reach under small dandelions without disturbing your ornamentals.

Garden fork: Essential for large taprooted weeds such as dock. Also useful for mild cases of quack grass.

Shovel: Best for thick sods of weeds that spread by runners. Cut a six-inch strip, then divide that into pieces. Lift and shake off the soil.

by planting some of the hardy annual flowers that act similarly. See Chapter 8 for a list of my favorites.

By thickly covering the ground with their own seedlings, these plants suppress most weeds. However, the ground needs to be clear before you sow. Any grass or dandelions present will continue to grow vigorously among your flowers, and picking them out later is both frustrating and time-consuming.

Remember that the key to dealing with weeds lies in respecting the need of the earth to be covered with a skin of growth. You, the gardener, have the privilege of making choices. Choose wisely, and nature will support you.

Chapter Nineteen

Worthy Opponents: Slugs, Rots, and Other Natural Disasters

In the world of plants, the probers, testers, and agents of destruction and removal of what isn't healthy are generally insects, munchers like slugs, and disease. It's sometimes hard for us to watch them and accept their role. We want to protect what we've planted, guard our investments, and fight back.

It's often easier to accept our own role as destroyer, making choices between petunias and dandelions, between "beneficial" and "destructive" beetles, than to accept nature's judgments. We curse and reach for the fungicide when a favorite tree comes down with leaf spot. We wage war in our gardens.

Having been taught to fight disease, we look upon wilts and rots as enemies. We perceive munchers like slugs as foes to be eradicated. It's time, though, for a change of view. It's natural to mourn a bit over the plants that didn't make it, but is death in the garden really a tragedy?

As always, a change of philosophy is worth many hours of yard work. One way to end the war with nature is to accept a common goal: strong, healthy, independent plants. Play with the vision of snails and blights as allies that can show you the weaknesses in your garden, the places other plants could fill better.

When your blue spruce loses half its needles to black aphids, perhaps what you're being told is, "This isn't the right place for this tree."

Perhaps the ground is too sandy and dry. Perhaps your house blocks the sun a spruce needs. You can either spend time and money fighting the aphids every year or start over with a tree better suited to your conditions.

Sometimes insects and disease are more like weeds, disfiguring but not fatal. Leaf spots may barely discolor the foliage, or they may turn entire sections of a tree brown. Aphids may curl some new growth but hardly affect the tree as a whole. Rabbits and deer may take a nibble here and there, or they may eat the lettuce to the ground and strip the roses of all their leaves. What can we live with, and what is too much to tolerate?

Tolerance and laziness fit well together, neither asking much effort. If you avoid a corner of the garden simply because you don't want to look at a plant attacked by aphids, you should probably do something about it. If you can eye it and speculate on how many ladybugs it's supporting, you're on your way to becoming an expert lazy gardener.

Insects often feed populations of birds, frogs, and other insects, serving purposes other than our own sense of fitness. Widening our perspective to include nature's viewpoint not only benefits the ecology, it keeps us from spending hours with pesticide and sprayer in hand.

DIAGNOSIS AND TREATMENT

How do you make the decision whether to indulge nature's processes or fight? First, look closely at the problem. What is really going on? Any plant under stress is vulnerable to attack by a number of problems, including predators like slugs and snails. Is the stress temporary, caused by recent transplanting? Can you nurse it through this bout, then leave it confidently alone?

Or is this problem caused by a misfit to environmental conditions, an intolerance for the drought or shade with which it has to contend? Can you, and do you want to, change these conditions?

As many as three-quarters of all plant problems can be traced to a difficulty in the environment. If you see brown or spotted leaves, wilting branches, or other disasters and can't see an obvious cause, consider overfertilization, a too-thick mulch, or even chemical spray burn as possible causes.

Are you dealing with unnatural predators such as Japanese beetles and European snails? These have no part in a balanced ecosystem here, having been released from normal controls existing in their native areas. Still, here there are, so what do you do about them?

Doing Nothing

In any of these situations, one possibility is simply to do nothing. Just watch what happens. Yes, the asparagus tips are getting eaten by the asparagus beetles. Watch. Yes, the slugs are eating holes in the hosta leaves. Watch. Admire the sensuous, slow, deliberate movements of the slugs.

Doing nothing may teach you many things. The tree whose leaves turned black and fell off may sprout new healthy growth. The second crop of strawberries may be untouched by rot. The hosta may be eaten to the ground. If you have a scientific bent to your curiosity, a longing to know "What happens if . . . ," this method is for you.

And, of course, you have the magnificent excuse of cooperating with nature to cover your natural inclination toward indolence. Your laziness is given respectability. How can you resist?

Doing Something

Perhaps it's the tree that shades your kitchen in summer that is under attack. Or the rhododendron given you as a wedding present that's dying. Perhaps you've always wanted fresh asparagus right out of your garden. You aren't willing to give up.

Certainly, newly transplanted specimens deserve some leeway, a bit of extra care and babying. You may try moving the plant around the yard to find a more congenial spot. You may go to the trouble of putting barriers around tiny marigolds and lettuce, protecting them from slugs.

If you're trying to save a favorite plant, you have several options. The first is physical removal of the pest. This could be through picking off, spraying with a strong stream of water, or creating some sort of barrier. Fences can keep deer, rabbits, and raccoons out. Gauzy films can protect vegetables from various maggots.

Live controls, predators eager to eat your pest, include ladybugs, trichogramma wasps, and lacewings; these can be ordered from companies specializing in organic gardening supplies. Healthy bird populations

What if Deer Are a Problem?

A really hungry deer will munch on almost any plant, but these are often avoided:

Strawberry tree (*Arbutus*), butterfly bush (*Buddleia*), *Calendula,* Mexican orange (*Choisya*), rock rose (*Cistus*), smokebush (*Cotinus*), foxglove (*Digitalis*), Lenten rose (*Helleborus orientalis*), *Iris,* juniper (*Juniperus*), lupine (*Lupinus*), Oregon grape (*Mahonia*), daffodil (*Narcissus*), Pacific wax myrtle (*Myrica*), oriental poppy (*Papaver orientale*), corn poppy (*Papaver rhoeas*), rosemary (*Rosmarinus*), gloriosa daisy (*Rudbeckia*), *Zinnia*

can also keep many insects under control. These aren't instant solutions; predators take time to build up a useful population. Don't use chemicals if you're trying this method, or you'll kill both the "good" and the "bad" insects.

A word about *Bacillus thuringinensis*, a popular organic control for destructive caterpillars: Don't assume it's totally benign. Many of the delicate butterflies we love are just as susceptible to its effects as the moths we're trying to eliminate. Use only if necessary, and then only on small areas.

The final weapon against pests and diseases are various chemicals. Certainly, they have their proper uses, but when you get to this point, be sure the trouble is worth the gain. Butterflies are extremely sensitive to any insecticide; much of the recent reduction of populations is because of pesticide use.

Use any pesticide, fungicide, or other chemical only when you absolutely must. If you need repeated applications each year, reconsider the possibility of replacing the afflicted tree or shrub with another.

DISEASE-RESISTANT PLANTS

Many disease-resistant varieties of fruits, berries, roses, and other plants have been developed in the past few decades. You can often get a potentially healthier variety if you're having trouble with an apple or pear tree, for instance.

State extension services spend much of their time testing new varieties of vegetables, fruits, and ornamentals. You may have picked out an old favorite for its familiar name, perhaps a Gravenstein apple because your grandmother had one whose fruit made great sauce. Yes, the taste was wonderful, but the tree gets scab nearly every year. Search out one of the new, unusual varieties. You may be able to visit an exhibition where samples of many apples are on display, ready for tasting. Often the flavor of an unknown is just as good and the tree less trouble to grow, an ideal solution for lazy gardeners.

Roses are notoriously time-consuming, often demanding fertilizer, pesticides, fungicides, and annual pruning. May I recommend David Austin English roses? Fragrant, tough, elegant, and gracefully branched, they seem to have everything going for them. Graced not with long-stemmed single blossoms but with clusters of full-petaled beauties, they have an old-fashioned form that charms almost everyone.

There are older varieties that have a toughness and disease resistance that might surprise you. One of my favorites is 'Queen Elizabeth', a clear pink whose bush has such vigor and energy that it's almost carefree.

Be sure to get local advice, however. What grows well in one section of the country may be a dud in another. Even a hundred miles may make a difference in the varieties that can be recommended.

In the end, resistant varieties are the answer. Plant the appropriate plant in the appropriate place and leave it alone. You'd be surprised at the number of varieties, species, and types of plants that would do well in your garden, if given a chance. You needn't fight a constant battle over something sickly and weak; why fight the process? Mourn and start over with something new.

Chapter Twenty

Tools for Pleasure

You're going to be using a number of tools, from hoses to pruning shears to trowels. You can find pleasure in handling them if you choose carefully. A well-balanced, well-crafted shovel can be a joy to use; a flimsy, poorly made one can be a source of frustration.

Tools mean work. If you are using one, it's because there is pruning, digging, mowing, transplanting, or weeding to be done. All you can do at this stage is make it as much fun as possible.

Tools in themselves are work. They need sharpening, oiling, protection from rain, and proper storage space. The best way to reduce their drain on your energy is to buy only what you need. What we own in some sense owns us, demanding our attention in some manner. What do you want to be owned by?

THE ESSENTIALS

Here are some tools I use in caring for my own and a few other people's gardens. I don't have a truck, so I make do with as little as possible.

First, I use a small duffel bag, about two feet long, for storing hand tools. I got a used one at a garage sale for two dollars, with zippered pockets at both ends. This keeps everything together in one place; when I garden, I simply carry the whole kit along.

Inside, I stow an apron with pockets—large ones at the bottom, small pencil pockets at the top. This lets me keep everything I need right at hand while I'm wandering around the garden. Nothing uses up more time than going back and forth for the pruning shears or the weeding knife. Things tend to get lost less frequently, too, if I can put them in pockets rather than down on the ground.

My most important hand tool is a good set of pruning shears. This is not the item to skimp on; get the best you can afford. Poor pruners soon become a frustration, binding when they should open or refusing to cut properly. Good ones feel balanced and effective, and are a pleasure to use.

Loppers are large pruning shears, suited to cutting inch-thick branches. If all your trees and shrubs are small, you probably won't need a pair right away. If you have just a few to cut, you can probably borrow one for a day or so. Don't invest in loppers until you're sure you'll use them regularly. Good ones aren't cheap, and poor ones are a nuisance.

A folding pruning saw is essential if you're going to be working with large shrubs or trees. It can substitute for loppers, if you don't have them, but tends to leave a ragged edge on small branches.

I have mixed feelings about gloves. I love the feel of digging into the ground with my unprotected hands, but as a musician I need clean fingernails and smooth skin. I love feeling the textures of leaves and bark, but need protection from scrapes and thorn scratches.

I've found that cloth gloves, while flexible and comfortable, wear out at the tips so quickly I can't use them. Leather is more expensive, but durable and an effective protection against thorns. Its thickness makes it a bit too stiff for comfort, however.

I've recently found some flexible, durable vinyl gloves, called "The Ultimate Glove,"™ with which I'm quite happy. A pair of these for ordinary work and a pair of leather gloves for dealing with spiky roses and blackberries are all I need.

A knife is my favorite tool for weeding. A sharpened triangular weeder works well also, and a trowel can serve double duty in weeding and in digging small holes. It can also loosen the soil around deep-rooted weeds like dandelions to help get them out.

A small pad of paper and a pen are useful tools. I keep them in my apron, ready for thoughts and inspirations that always seem to surface during idle time in the garden, moments when I'm just sitting back enjoying the sun or watching butterflies.

My duffel bag also provides storage for a variety of other odds and ends, including twine and plastic tape for tying up vines, a small bottle of starting solution and another of liquid fertilizer, and some knee pads given to me by a generous client. You may not need all of these. Just remember to keep all your bits and pieces together in a similar fashion so you can find them when needed.

Finding is a major problem with small tools, not just in an over-crowded garage, but under bushes and among the ground cover you weeded yesterday. My solution is to spray the handles of my weeding knives with orange paint. Some tools come in red or orange, but if they don't, I highly recommend changing their original color to a brighter one.

When it comes to larger tools, a round, pointed shovel and a digging fork take care of most needs. The shovel can move gravel or a small tree. The fork is needed for loosening soil in planting holes and lifting out quack grass. Yes, there are other shapes and sizes of shovels, but unless you have a specific job requiring them, skip the expense.

While I usually recommend the best-quality tool, here I go for the cheap ones. Why? Because they're usually lighter, and I see no reason to expend energy on lifting metal as well as soil. None of mine have broken yet.

One of my favorite tools is called a Winged Weeder™. A combination hoe and sharp-pointed prying tool, it's much lighter and easier to use than conventional hoes. Invaluable for keeping large areas of mulch clear, it obliterates weed seedlings with a few passes back and forth just beneath the soil surface. It can also be used to pull up slightly larger weeds without bending over.

Shovel, spades, hoes, and trowels all work better when sharpened occasionally. A small flat file, stored in your duffel bag until needed, handles this job easily. Simply file one side of the tool's edge to an acute angle. You'll be surprised at how much easier cutting roots or sod becomes after sharpening, amply repaying the small trouble required.

When it comes to Rototillers and other machines, consider whether you want to buy or just rent whenever you need one. Tool rental stores have excellent selections of brush cutters, large Rototillers, and other useful devices, probably of better quality than you'd buy yourself. You might also be able to borrow what you need from a friend. Not buying unless you have to saves space and maintenance time, as well as money.

A word about hoses: Perhaps only someone who has spent hours and hours of the summer watering plants at a nursery can appreciate the good qualities of a hose, but to me, using an excellent hose is sheer pleasure. No kinks, no twisting, no running back and forth straightening out tangles. Buy the best.

BUDGETING FOR TOOLS

How can you afford to purchase the best tools? Don't buy one unless you really need it. Resist the sales and the bargain stores at first. If you want to shop around, go to the quality places first, such as a nursery near a wealthy suburb.

Leave your checkbook and credit cards behind; this trip is just for the sake of research. You'll see the best, perhaps fall in love with the way a certain pruning shear fits your hands. Now go back to one of the discount stores and look again. Can you get the same brand or the same quality at a lower price?

Another idea is to share tools with a friend. After all, how often do you use a pair of loppers? Once a year? Twice? Perhaps you could buy the loppers and your friend could buy a great digging fork. If you make a point of returning tools cleaned, sharpened (if needed), and in good condition, the system will work.

A few good tools are worth a garage full of poor ones, both in the pleasure you receive from using them and in the quality of work you can accomplish. Put off buying the new shirt you don't really need and spend the money on a tool that will make your gardening a pleasure.

ARRANGING YOUR STORAGE SPACE

What if you already have a full garage? Yard sales, gifts to worthy friends and thrift stores, or simply tossing unneeded items in the garbage will all reduce your load. Is there anything you haven't used in the last year? Get rid of it. Is there anything you don't really like but feel obligated to use? Get rid of it.

And while you're at it, clean out the rest of your garage or tool shed. Old pots, half-used bags of fertilizer, packets of seeds you meant to sow but didn't, netting tossed in a corner—get rid of whatever you're just keeping around. Each unnecessary tool or gadget is a burden. How can you expect to trim your gardening time down to a minimum when you spend half an hour looking for the trowel you threw in there a month ago?

Now, have some fun with your dull tool shed. Paint is cheap, and you may even have some bright colors left over from an indoor project. Why not paint sunflowers on the walls? Or let your kids loose on the door? Who says tool sheds need to be sober and businesslike?

Use odds and ends of paint to brighten the handles of small, easily misplaced tools. Paint the shelves yellow and the floor lime green. Who is going to see this excess of enthusiasm but you and your family?

Now you have a colorful storage space, a small duffel bag for hand tools, and a minimum number of larger ones. May your stripped-down set of tools have as lazy a life as you do!

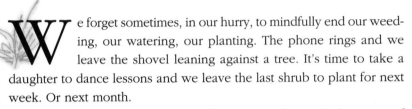

Epilogue

Endings and Conclusions

We forget sometimes, in our hurry, to mindfully end our weeding, our watering, our planting. The phone rings and we leave the shovel leaning against a tree. It's time to take a daughter to dance lessons and we leave the last shrub to plant for next week. Or next month.

Well, you say, that's the way life is, one thing piled on top of another. Who has time to stand back and reflect on what they've done?

A pity, really. There's no roundness, no wholeness, in moving past the end of an activity, a job, a relationship, without noticing it's passing. We're on to the next, still carrying leftovers from what has passed.

Perhaps that is the problem. We never stop to put down the burdens we carry from spending time at work, washing dishes, in the garden. The frustration with the boss's pet project, anger at someone who failed to help dry the dishes, and worries about a rose with mildew stay with us just as the shovel we left out stays with us.

How long does it take to drop the past? Perhaps only seconds if you're ending a bout of weeding. Just long enough to stand back and admire the brown, freshly cleared soil, to be grateful for the opportunity to feel the wind on your skin, the warm sun on your back. Thankfulness is the best tonic for our souls.

We also need to congratulate ourselves on our work, celebrate the new bed of wildflowers, honor the bit of weeding we managed to squeeze in between appointments. How can we enjoy our accomplishments if we don't stop to notice them?

Of course, at the same time, we can be putting away tools, lining up plants in pots for the next session of gardening, sweeping the dirt off the front porch. Little rituals, trivial perhaps, but effective in helping us end with mindfulness.

Do I actually do all this myself? Yes and no. I'm as scattered as everyone else, but I'm experimenting, occasionally, with finality. Being a chronic misplacer of tools, I'm trying to use closure as a way to keep things ordered. I rebel against childhood messages of "pick it up, put it away," but admit that life would be easier if I did. Piggybacking praise and duty helps me stay happy and organized.

As a musician, I also experiment with music, using a few pennywhistle pieces to both open and close my time in the garden. I notice a sense of calmness and relaxation when I do.

I experiment with giving thanks for the butterfly that wandered by, the frog that visited, the velvety iris petals, and dramatic leaves. Barely fifteen seconds of silent thanks seems to clear my heart.

Sometimes endings involve grieving. Is grief really too strong a word for what we feel when the apple tree we planted so hopefully dies? Or when we find a dead nestling with its parents calling loudly nearby? Conclusions allow us to clear these moments also.

Worse, perhaps, are the moments of guilt when we recognize how much we failed to do, how the newly planted penstemon died because we forgot to water it during a hot spell. Perhaps just saying out loud how sorry we are will help us to drop the guilt and come back to the garden with new enthusiasm next time.

Enthusiasm. That's the key to endings and beginnings. As lazy gardeners we need to cultivate it, nurture it, coddle it. If we can leave the garden with enthusiasm, we can return in the same spirit. Not to push ourselves into more and more projects, but to enjoy our gardens more deeply, more restfully, with a softness for ourselves and all of nature.

Thank you for joining me in this exploration of lazy gardening, a partnership with nature. May you spend little time on your knees pulling weeds—and many hours sitting in the sun with good friends, sipping wine, watching the swallows dart across your flowery lawn.

Index

Hosta (*Hosta*), 37, 113
Hummingbirds,
  rufous, 77
Humulus japonicus, 43
Hyssop, dwarf
  (*Hyssopus*), 43

Iberis
  coronaria, 56
  sempervirens, 32
Ice plant, 50
Immediate gratification,
  93–95
Impatiens, 109
Iris (*Iris*), 51, 132
  bearded, 14, 22
  pseudacorus, 22, 59
  Siberian (*sibirica*),
    58, 108
Ivy
  English, 48, 49
  Kenilworth, 55

Japanese anemone, 32,
  51, 58, 60
Japanese hop, 43
Jasminum nudiflorum,
  32, 50, 64
Jerusalem artichokes, 69
Junipers (*Juniperus*),
  37, 43, 64, 109, 132
  chinensis
    'Columnaris', 43
  conferta, 50
  scopulorum 'Blue
    Haven', 43
  shore (*horizontalis*
    'Bar Harbor'), 50

Kale, 69, 72
Kalmia, 13
Kinnikinick, 22, 38, 48,
  49, 64, 109
Klamath weed, 126

Lady's mantle, 22
Lamb's ears, 37, 59, 60
Lamium maculatum, 48
Larkspur, 55, 56, 66
Lavender cotton, 64
Layering, 109
Layia elegans, 56
Lenten rose, 32, 56, 132
Lettuce, 70, 72
Light, 11–12
  plants for sun, 22
Lily-of-the-valley, 32
Limnanthes douglasii, 56
Linarea purpurea, 59
Lingonberry, 22
Linum
  grandiflorum
    'Rubrum', 56
  perenne, 22
Liquidambar, 22
Lobelia, trailing, 113
Lobelia cardinalis
  (cardinal flower),
    22, 59
Lobularia, 55
Lonicera, 43, 49
  japonica 'Halliana', 48
Love-in-a-mist, 32, 54
Lupine (*Lupinus*), 56, 132
Lychnis coronaria, 32,
  56, 59

Maclaya, 66
Mahonia (*Mahonia*),
  22, 132
  creeping (*repens*), 64
  long-leaf (*nervosa*), 50
Mallow (*Malva*), 66
  pink (*alcea
    fastigiata*), 56,
    58–59
Maples, 31, 79
Marigolds, 55
Marsh mallow, 73

Marsh marigold, 22, 59
Meadow rue, 56, 59, 66
Meadows
  wildlife and, 78–79
Meconopsis cambrica,
  56, 61, 73
Medicago sativa, 112
Mentha, 22
  requienii, 37
*Mesembryanthemum
  crystallinum*, 50
Mexican orange, 132
Mignonette, 56
Mimulus, 22
Miner's lettuce, 72
Mint, 22, 60, 73
Mirabilis, 55
Monarda didyma, 32
Monkey flower, 22
Monkshood, 59, 66
Montia, 72
Morning glory, 125
Mountain bluet, 57, 60
Mulches, 17, 18, 46–47
Mullein, 56
Muscari, 32
Mustard, 112
Myosotis, 55
Myrica, 22, 132
Myrtle, Pacific wax, 132

Narcissus, 61, 132
Nasturtiums, 54
Natural Garden, The
  (Druse), 32
Nemophila, 55
Nettles, 72, 126
Nicotiana, 66
Nigella, 32, 54
  'Miss Jekyll', 54
Nyssa sylvatica, 66

Oak, English, 30
Oats, 112